Advance Praise for *Homegrown Faith*

"To grow through the Church year with Heidi Bratton is to see Truth revealed by the most ordinary things and events of day-to-day home life—a ringing alarm clock, a missed cup of coffee, a pot of boiling water… and it is especially to see how grace is revealed by the most extraordinary things—those eternal beings we sleep, play, eat, and argue with, that collection of souls that God has assembled into a family. Best of all, *Homegrown Faith* does not stay home; it moves out in mission—to foreign countries, to engage our separated brethren, to change the world. A year spent with Heidi will grow faith in your home —and beyond."

—MRS. MARY KOCHAN, editor in chief, Catholic Lane, catholiclane.com

"Like your mom's best recipes, Heidi Bratton's *Homegrown Faith* is the ideal tool to help any home create the perfect blend of faith, family, and fun. Take Heidi's wisdom, her wonderful personal reflections, and her terrific ideas for bringing the faith to life in your home, blend in your own unique mix of characters and life circumstances and you'll have the blueprint for a liturgical year filled with precious memories and new traditions."

—LISA M. HENDEY, founder and editor of CatholicMom.com

a   ~~*h~lic Moms

"Heidi Bratton relates the real experiences of an outstanding Catholic wife and mother of six. She gives good insights, offers practical wisdom, and provides an "inside look" into the working of what has been called 'the domestic church,' humorously interpreting the ordinary events of a contemporary household with the eyes of faith. The inclusion of discussion questions will help readers to see Christ in the context of family life and encourage the formation of the deeper, more personal faith in our Lord. Finally, the book's arrangement according to the Church's liturgical year gives it a further catechetical dimension. I do not hesitate to recommend highly this enjoyable and helpful book to others!"

—GEORGE W. COLEMAN, Bishop of Fall River, Massachusetts

"God speaks to us in so many ways each day, but many of us have not yet learned to listen to what he says through these daily events. Heidi Bratton does us all a favor in this excellent book by helping us tune into God's frequency, and derive life-changing lessons, from the ordinary events of day-to-day life. This will be an inspirational read for parents seeking to make their home a domestic church through the often chaotic liturgy of family life. This is also an accessible, inspiring, and transformative read for younger Catholics raised in a post-Christian culture, who will discover how to look at life through the sacramental mindset that flows from our faith. *Homegrown Faith* will help every reader's faith grow."

—FR. ROGER J. LANDRY, executive editor of *The Anchor*

"'Take small bites and keep on chewing.' This homespun wisdom summarizes very well this little book of meditations to guide you through the Church year. From the winter of Advent and Christmas to the springtime of Lent and Easter and the verdant growth of Ordinary Time, each of the fifty-two chapters offers encouragement to the Catholic mother's heart, helping her to grow in godliness and peace. Weekly meditations combined with daily ponderings makes this perfect for individual or group meditations."

—HEIDI HESS SAXTON, founder, Extraordinary Moms Network and author
of *Raising Up Mommy: Virtues for Difficult Mothering Moments*

"As an involved mother of seven, my days are jam-packed. If I do find a precious moment to read for my own edification, I look for a spiritual pick-me-up, a tonic for my soul that will shore up my drooping shoulders and set my feet back on solid ground. Heidi Bratton's funny, poignant anecdotes from her own life help me to see my family, my circumstances—and yes, even my own foibles—in a way that encourages me to see ordinary events as priceless opportunities to love. Heidi's words will ring true to any woman whose heart is in need of refreshment."

—MARIE THIBODEAU, cofounder of the Little Daughters of the Sacred Heart

"I am a young Catholic mother—just starting our family—and I absolutely loved this book! I loved the way the book is set up to facilitate prayer life, whether personal or group, throughout the year. I guess finding time for prayer and connecting everyday life to God is something that I think every parent, upon entering parenthood, struggles with. *Homegrown Faith* is very helpful in this way. Heidi Bratton is a wonderful role model to people like me who really want to be good Catholic parents—with our society that can be so distracting, her message is so encouraging!"

—BECKY SHARKEY, volunteer for Prolife Across America

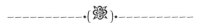

"*Homegrown Faith: Nurturing Your Catholic Family* is a delightful book filled with simple, real-life anecdotes that point to deeper spiritual truths. Author Heidi Bratton doesn't just talk theoretically about faith and family life, she lives it! I highly recommend this book for couples just embarking on the journey of parenthood and also for parents who have been at it a while and need the encouragement, refreshment, and inspiration necessary to finish a marathon"

—DEBRA HERBECK, speaker and author of
Safely Through the Storm: 120 Reflections on Hope

FABRA

Heidi Bratton

homegrown *Faith*

nurturing
your
CATHOLIC
FAMILY

INTRODUCTION BY Cardinal Seán P. O'Malley

Family Resources Center
415 NE Monroe,
Peoria, IL 61603 (309) 839-2287

SERVANT
BOOKS

PUBLISHED BY ST. ANTHONY MESSENGER PRESS
CINCINNATI, OHIO

Scripture quotations, unless otherwise noted, are taken from *The Holy Bible,
Revised Standard Version, Catholic Edition,* copyright © 1966 by Division of
Christian Education of the National Council of the Churches in Christ in the
United States of America. Used by permission. All rights reserved.
Quotations are taken from "The Summons" by John L. Bell, copyright © 1987,
Wild Goose Resource Group, Iona Community, Scotland. GIA Publications, Inc.,
exclusive North American agent, 7404 S. Mason Ave., Chicago, IL 60638.
www.giamusic.com. 800.442.1358. All rights reserved. Used by permission.

Cover and interior design by Mark Sullivan
Cover image ©Ocean Photography | Veer

LIBRARY OF CONGRESS CATALOGING-IN-PUBLICATION DATA
Bratton, Heidi.
Homegrown faith : nurturing your Catholic family / Heidi Bratton ; introduction
by Sean P. O'Malley.
p. cm.
ISBN 978-1-61636-134-1 (acid-free paper)
1. Mothers—Prayers and devotions. 2. Catholic Church—Prayers and devotions. 3. Church year meditations. I. Title.
BX2170.M65B73 2011
248.8'431—dc23
2011025810

ISBN 978-1-61636-134-1

Published by Servant Books
an imprint of St. Anthony Messenger Press
28 W. Liberty St.
Cincinnati, OH 45202
www.AmericanCatholic.org
www.ServantBooks.org

Printed in the United States of America.
Printed on acid-free paper.
11 12 13 14 15 5 4 3 2 1

----------•(✿)•----------

Contents

----------•(✿)•----------

Acknowledgments

Although the idea for this particular book gestated on my computer for longer than it takes an elephant baby to spring forth from its mother, I am most grateful for the time it gave me to include in these pages the recent adventure of being pregnant and delivering our sixth child at age forty-one. Born eighteen years after his oldest sibling, the arrival of little Jesse has softened and reshaped my mothering heart all over again. Thank you, Jesse "Bear"; this one is for you!

In my worst moments, I look up to heaven and cry, "Why, oh God, can't I have even a little bit of uninterrupted time to write?" Then, in my best moments, I realize that without the material provided to me by my husband and our six children, I'd have nothing to write about. And so it is with a humble heart that I acknowledge and offer thanks to the inner circle, to those who have given me not only so much material, but also the time to write it all down in (mostly) cohesive sentences.

Thank you to my husband, John, for his the unwavering support and 1:00 AM edits. You are the "invisible" man who makes my work look good. Credit for this book actually seeing the light of day goes to our middle children, Lucy and Benjamin. You guys are champion babysitters! If not for the prayer support and two thumbs-up given to me by my three oldest children, Nicole, Peter, and Olivia, I'd be stalled out on page one. Thank you each for letting me share our stories!

Two editors in particular have trusted me with the readership of their publications: my *Anchor* newspaper editor, Fr. Roger Landry, and Mary Kochan of the Catholic Lane website. Thank you both for your spiritual backing and for the confidence you've shown in my mission to bring Catholic families closer to God and to each other. A third editor, Claudia Volkman of Servant Books, is, hands-down, the most encouraging, most multitalented person I have met in the wide world of publishing. Thank you, Claudia, for blessing me with your friendship and for nourishing my work with your faith, your abilities, and your enthusiasm.

Lastly, to Our Almighty God be all the glory, honor, and power, now and forever. Amen.

Foreword

Danielle Bean

Hello, my name is Danielle Bean, and I am a recovering "Catholic mom program" addict. I have a secret closet filled with abandoned study guides, calendars, chore charts, spiritual makeovers, homemaking planners, and self-improvement manuals.

Each of these resources has been helpful for a short while and inspiring in its own way, but in the end I wound up feeling like I "failed" every one of these programs for authentic and organized Christian living.

But then again, perhaps they have failed me.

There is no cure-all for the unique challenges of faithful family living, and books and programs that set up grand expectations of living "happily ever after" are bound to disappoint.

That is why I sincerely appreciate *Homegrown Faith*. It is simple and organized. It is chock-full of a year's worth of good ideas and encouraging words, but it is humble too. This book doesn't pretend to be a cure-all. It doesn't set up unrealistic expectations. It only gently offers support, inspiration, and encouragement to Catholic women as they seek to build the kingdom of God, beginning with their own domestic churches.

I first met Heidi Bratton during an Advent-themed "Faith & Family" podcast we recorded together in late 2009. We spent about thirty minutes chatting on the phone and by the time I hung up, I was hooked. On her cheerful demeanor. On her down-to-earth sense of humor. On her commitment to family life. And on her generous sharing of her love for the Catholic faith.

All of these personal qualities are what make the work Heidi has done in *Homegrown Faith* such a treasure for Catholic moms and their families. Here in these pages, we have inspiration at the ready, practical tips for raising kids on fire with their faith, and a handbook for Catholic family life—all steeped in Scripture and rounded out with amusing anecdotes and a healthy dash of realism.

You will not fail *Homegrown Faith*. You will succeed.

In whatever way you choose to do the "program" Heidi shares here, these heartfelt pages have the power to move you and your family closer to Christ and help you grow in your love for one another. How much more successful could any of us desire to be?

I leaf through these pages and find myself eagerly anticipating a year of faith. A year of family. A year of moving myself and others closer to heaven, day by day. Heidi has mapped out the way and invites us to choose to live joyfully along with her—to succeed and fail, fall down and get back up again—always keeping our eyes on Christ.

God calls every one of us and our families closer to him through the lovely pages of this "homegrown" book. I hope you'll join us as we spend some time together here and find out what he has to say.

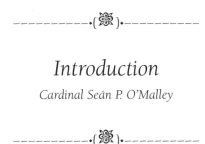

Introduction

Cardinal Seán P. O'Malley

Amid a society that values individual rights and entitlements over and above self-giving and sacrifice, it can be very challenging to chart a course for authentic family life. Through this wonderful book, *Homegrown Faith*, Heidi Bratton's reflections provide a resource that will help to bring strengthened faith and genuine happiness to all families.

Our Holy Father, Pope Benedict XVI, during the course of his visit to the United States in 2008, noted that through family life we experience "the fundamental elements of peace: justice and love." In addition, the Pope noted our responsibility to promote the values which enable the human person to flourish and reminded us that it is the unique responsibility of parents to firmly plant and nurture those moral values in their homes. By way of *Homegrown Faith*, Heidi Bratton makes an important contribution to this mission, providing the opportunity for families to come together in prayer and to recognize the many blessings they share, even in the midst of the inevitable challenges.

In addition to making *Homegrown Faith* part of your personal spiritual reading, I encourage you to consider this book as a gift for your relative and friends who are raising families or spend time with their extended families. We are all called to be disciples of the Lord and that work includes sharing spiritual encouragement with others. The reflections contained in *Homegrown Faith* are an excellent means of building up the Church one family at a time; this book would surely be well received in any home where people seek to grow closer to one another by developing a closer relationship with Jesus Christ.

Cardinal Seán P. O'Malley
Archbishop of Boston
Member of the Presidential Council of the Pontifical Council for the Family
October, 2010

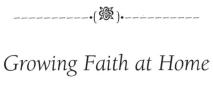

Growing Faith at Home

"Homegrown." "Handpicked." "Native Produce." Signs like this dot the roadside when sticky, hot August rolls into cool, crisp September. Ask anyone in my family and they'll tell you that early autumn is my favorite time of year. Why? Because I absolutely love farmer's markets, roadside stands, and "U-Pick" produce! In an age of mass production and slick marketing schemes, hand-painted roadside signs like these attract my attention. First of all, it must be admitted that this attraction comes from the fact that I have a fruit tooth as well as a sweet tooth. Such signs also let me know that whatever is being produced has been chosen carefully and tended with love.

Chosen carefully and tended with love: this is the same way I would describe how to produce a faith-filled Catholic family in any season, simple as it may sound. This book, then, has two very down-to-earth objectives: 1) helping parents choose simple yet meaningful ways of living and teaching the Catholic faith at home, and 2) helping them better understand and tend to the Scriptural and sacramental life offered to them by the universal Catholic Church. Put together, I believe these two goals will provide the nutrient-rich soil and the life-giving water necessary for growing a faith-filled, Catholic family.

Throughout this book, readers will find the recurring idea that faith is more often caught than it is taught; additionally, even when it is taught, I believe we can only effectively teach that which we love. This being the case, some of the devotions in this book are aimed specifically at helping moms and dads grow in their love and understanding of Jesus Christ and the Catholic Church. The principle of faith here is the same as that of an airplane oxygen mask—we need to put our own on first, and then we'll be able to help those around us.

Some of the reflections in this book are written to provide new ideas for family life and child raising that are truly and uniquely Catholic. This is not, however, a how-to book on parenting. When we talk about things as personal as parenting styles, holiday traditions, or what time to attend Mass, I think the Catholic tent is really quite roomy, capable of hosting diverse devotions within the same doctrine. Spiritualities as diverse as charismatic and contemplative or music as varied as Gregorian chant and contemporary Christian rock can and do thrive under the one doctrinal umbrella of the Catholic creed.

We can, therefore, have a lot of fun discovering what parish activities, outside ministries, forms of evangelism, and even historical celebrations work for the individuals in our homes. The recurring theme here is to get engaged and stay engaged with our Catholic faith and with our family members in meaningful ways. This book will recommend tested ways of making faith in Jesus Christ real and relevant to our children through the sharing of humorous short stories and analogies that illuminate scriptural truths.

I do want readers to know from the beginning that I am neither a theologian nor an expert in Christianity. I am simply a committed Catholic Christian woman. The titles I am most proud of aren't dazzling at all; they are "Mrs." and "Mom," and they also describe the duties that occupy the majority of my time. Yet, inasmuch as God has primarily called me to the vocations of marriage and motherhood, he has also given me lifelong passions for photography, writing, and teaching, and I am, therefore, grateful for the opportunities I've been given to share an insight or two with others on how to tend to the faith life of a family with loving care.

A few tidbits about myself: My husband, John, and I are both cradle-turned-committed Catholics. As do farmers with their crops, John and I have experienced fruitful seasons and barren seasons over our twenty-two years of married life. We sprouted a nearly instant family by having five children in eight years immediately after saying "I do." The fatigue of that planting season crossed seamlessly into the frantic family phase of having toddlers and school-aged children, all of whom needed as much diligent watering and weeding as do window boxes in June. Then, eighteen years after baby number one and ten years after baby number five, God awarded us with a huge bonus: baby number six! We are now in the family season of all six children maturing as rapidly as bean sprouts in July. With the oldest children heading off to college, and the youngest still working his way through his round of "firsts" with talking and walking, my husband and I are really spanning the gamut of parenting right now. We are enjoying every minute of watching God direct the oldest ones to green pastures of their own while still having a baby at home to cuddle and rock to sleep. Okay, okay, I'm not enjoying every minute of watching the oldest ones venture off on their own; I miss them terribly, but what a thrill to watch the ripening of their own gifts and talents.

There is more, and I'll be sharing my love of Jesus and family life throughout these pages, but that's enough for now. The kids are mixing up some cookie dough in the kitchen, and I think they could really use a taste tester.

Heidi Bratton
Ann Arbor, Michigan
August 2011

Using This Book for Personal or Group Devotions

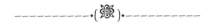

For the special purpose of guiding readers through a year's worth of spiritual growth, this book corresponds to the liturgical year of the Catholic Church and the four seasons of nature. Beginning with the first Sunday of Advent, the fifty-two reflections in this book are ordered topically with one for every week of the year.

Each reflection is followed by four questions or activities to prompt personal, spiritual reflections. The reflection of the week is meant to be read on Monday. The four spiritual prompts that follow are designed to be used one at a time for the other four weekdays. Having only five days of reading and reflecting each week, rather than seven, will leave you with time for the Mass readings and other spiritually enriching activities on the weekends without having that awful feeling of having to hurry through or skip over things in order to keep pace each week.

However, it's your book! Read it all at once and then go back over specific reflections that you'd like to dig into a little further, jump around, or begin reading in whatever season you'd like. No matter in what order you enjoy the individual reflections, you can maximize their content by using the four questions that follow as prompts for personal prayer or as guides for discussion in a weekly study group. You will need to have on hand a Bible (a Catholic study Bible would be most helpful), a copy of the *Catechism of the Catholic Church*, a journal, and a pen or pencil.

Using This Book for Personal Daily Prayer

Daily prayer is the meat and potatoes of our personal relationship with God, but it can be really tough to maintain amid the scramble of family life. A couple of helpful hints I've discovered after years of well-intended but failed attempts at establishing a personal prayer time:

1. Try to select one time during the day and one place where you will always pray. Keep this book and all supporting material together in that one place, perhaps in a pretty bag or basket, so you do not have to waste precious time looking for them each day.

2. Routine and discipline are the keys to developing a consistent prayer time. Just do it!

3. A good sprint is better than no marathon at all. Getting ten to fifteen minutes a day to read, to pray, and to journal your thoughts alone is no small feat. For this reason, the daily Scripture readings and questions following each devotional are short. If you finish them and still

have more time alone, then let the Holy Spirit do the talking by sitting in silence and listening for any further inspiration on the topic of the day. Be prepared, however, to be blessed with more than ten or fifteen minute's worth of inspiration. Seriously, it is an amazing principle of spiritual multiplication that as we develop the habit of spending time with God on a daily basis, the Holy Spirit whispers into our ears further wisdom and understanding as we go about the rest of our day.

To begin each day:

1. Begin with a prayer inviting the Holy Spirit to guide and inspire you.

2. Read that day's reading, or select one of the four reflection questions or Scriptures that follow. Then spend time prayerfully considering the day's reading or question and journal your thoughts.

3. End with a prayer of thanksgiving for this time with God, and invite the Holy Spirit to be with you and your family during the rest of the day.

Don't worry if a child or two clamors for attention or climbs into your lap while you try to pray. Holiness is attractive. Your children will naturally desire to be with you as you pray. If they do join you, set and reinforce firm guidelines of quietness so you can continue, but don't try to stretch your prayer time too long. It will only make your (and their) patience wear thin. God will reward your efforts as you model to your children how to have a personal prayer time each day.

Using this Book as a Guide for Group Prayer

If you will be using this book in a group setting, be sure to complete the reading and questions yourself before getting together with the group. Flying by the seat of your pants is okay on occasion, but being prepared is generally more helpful to everyone. To begin each gathering:

1. Appoint one person to pose the questions, facilitate the discussion, and keep the conversation moving and on topic.

2. Open by praying (singing a hymn together is a great way to pray in unison) and inviting the Holy Spirit to guide and inspire your discussion.

3. Be sensitive to the facilitator's promptings, staying on topic, and each member's honest sharing. Be careful not to hog all the airtime or misuse the gathering to gossip or air unrelated grievances or inappropriate information. Focus on encouraging and lifting one another up to God.

4. Appoint a member to seek expert counsel on behalf of the group if questions are raised that cannot be answered within the group, especially those related to questions of scriptural meaning and Catholic teaching.

5. End by praying for one another's needs and with thanksgiving for the time to gather as the Body of Christ.

---------•(✿)•---------

Feasting on Faith at Home:
Reflections for Advent, Christmas, and Ordinary Time in Winter

---------•(✿)•---------

Seek After Joy

I don't think of myself as a crabby person. As a matter a fact, when I was younger, I had more than a few coworkers tell me I was a little too happy. In particular, I remember working as a chef's assistant in college. After working the 5:00 AM shift for an entire semester, the chef, an older lady, requested that I be relocated as far away from her as possible. She mumbled something to our supervisor about my cheeriness giving her a headache at that time of the morning. She was my standing image of a really crabby person...until I aged a few years myself.

Nowadays, it seems that I wake up my same cheery self, but before I even get out of bed something comes along to make me crabby. Like the alarm clock. It's really irritating to start the day behind schedule because it went off late...again. And when it does go off on time, does it really have to be so loud?

And what's the deal with the hot water heater not keeping up with several showers in a row? It's really irksome to be behind schedule because the alarm didn't go off, to have one of the kids jump in the shower before me, and then to have my shower run cold right in the middle. If all these irritating things would stop happening to me, then my family could see what a truly positive person I am.

Oh, and how I behaved yesterday? That crabbiness was not my fault. I was patient all day. I put the kids on time-outs instead of yelling, even when one threw a wooden block at another who was screaming bloody murder, but I won't mention any names here in print. I entertained hungry younger kids in the car during sports practices for the older kids. I kept dinner warm for a certain someone who arrived home late, no name mentioned. I didn't even hang up on the telemarketer selling light bulbs!

In short, I bit my tongue, kept my cool, and counted to ten all day. But when I backed out of the driveway and heard that plastic crunch under my wheels, well, that was it. That crabbiness was long overdue, even if the whole neighborhood heard about it.

So what's a Catholic mom to do? I don't seem to get a minute to be cheery before something irritating happens to rob me of my joy. Lately, I've been a little afraid that I may be turning into that crabby cafeteria lady. Well, the solution to my dilemma came on the lips of a similarly overwhelmed Catholic friend. While chatting about kids and family life, she mentioned that lately she had been trying to "seek after joy." I had never heard that phrase before, but it was as if Jesus himself had whispered it from heaven.

Sometimes joy comes naturally. Sometimes it does not. But real joy, like real love, is not found in the absence of frustrations or in ongoing, happy events. The kind of joy Jesus offers his followers is the fruit of much watering, weeding, fertilizing, and maybe even some pruning. Real joy is rooted in knowing Jesus as Lord and Savior, because compared to the joy of sharing eternal life with him everything else is truly temporary. Our joy in the Lord may not always be in full bloom, but we can choose to seek after and cultivate it.

St. Paul writes in Galatians 5:22–23 that joy is one of the fruits of the humble desire to "live by the Spirit," and thereby to grow in all of the fruit of the Spirit, which he lists as "love, joy, peace, patience, kindness, goodness, faithfulness, gentleness, self-control." Yup—my parenting could use a good dose of that list. I think I'll write my friend's words, "Seek after joy," in lipstick on my mirror so I'll be reminded of them first thing every morning, right after the sweet sound of my alarm clock.

Growing Spiritually This Week

1. Read Galatians 5:16–26. List the "acts of the sinful nature" (typically called vices) in these verses that are holding you back from experiencing true joy. Which of these are standing in the way of joy in your life?

2. Read Galatians 5:16–26. We cannot manufacture the fruit of the Spirit (verse 22) in our lives. They are by-products of living by the Spirit (verse 24–25). Review your list from Question 1. Which vices or personal stresses are the biggest obstacles to joy in your life today? How could you remove them?

3. Sketch a picture of yourself being "in step" with the Spirit (Galatians 5:25).

4. Read Galatians 5:16–26. How would you define the phrase "seek after joy"?

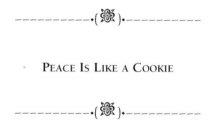

Peace Is Like a Cookie

Peace is like a cookie. Peace is a result, a final product, not a raw ingredient. How do I know this? Well, because in trying to create peace, I have never been able to do so in the absence of faith, hope, love, and a few other specialized virtues. The comparison to cookies is an easy leap, then, because you can't make cookies without some basic raw ingredients like butter, sugar, eggs, plus a few other specialized ingredients. Peace is like a cookie.

I started my quest to understand what "peace" was when my teenage son asked me if I thought peace was possible in the Middle East. I answered him, like a good lawyer, by stalling: "Well, that depends on what you mean by peace." Like all clever teens, he raised his eyebrows and replied, "You know, Mom. Peace, as in no war." So much for my legal career.

His question was brought on by the deluge of Christmas cards wishing everyone peace, secular holiday songs prattling on about the idea of peace on earth without any moral context, and the continued unrest in the Middle East. In these contexts, peace was being worshiped as the zenith of all human desire, worshiped with the devotion that Christians are supposed to offer to God alone. In these settings, peace is venerated as the bandage of choice for all the world's ills. But if that is true, why such a bad adhesive? Through the centuries and across all cultures, why doesn't peace stick?

My son and I mused further, only to find that the whole concept of peace was so nebulous as to be meaningless. We tried hard to identify the single most important ingredient of peace, but we couldn't. We had to conclude that peace simply isn't a stand-alone deal. Without unselfish love, peace isn't possible between two people, much less nations of people. Without hope that difficult times will get better, peace fades as quickly as it sparks. Without convicted faith that in the end good will prevail over evil, those who labor for peace only look suicidal. And yet Jesus himself, following the custom of the Jewish people, kept greeting people with "Shalom," meaning "Peace be with you." Peace, therefore, just couldn't be as impossible as it seemed to be to my son and me.

All of which makes me think of cookies. Before I am able to serve up and savor a warm plateful, I have to obtain the right ingredients, measure them out in the right proportions for the type of cookie I want, and mix the ingredients together for just the right amount of time. Several weeks ago, we baked a few hundred cookies. To celebrate St. Lucy's Day (December 13th) we usually bake and give Christmas cookies to our friends and neighbors with a Christmas card. During that bake-a-thon, I found myself mulling over the conversation I had with my son about peace, and I wondered which ingredient of the cookies being baked was the most important. Then, smack in the middle of pressing a Hershey's Kiss into a warm ball of just-baked peanut-butter dough, the answer hit me. The most important thing wasn't an ingredient. It was the heat! I can mix together and roll into little balls all the ingredients I want, but without heat, I will never have a cookie.

And so it is with peace. Jesus is the most important element of peace. Without Jesus, we can roll together as many virtues and good intentions, wishes and works as we want, but we will never have peace. Jesus told his disciples in John 14:27, "Peace I leave with you; my peace I give to you; not as the world gives do I give to you. Let not your hearts be troubled, neither let them be afraid." In other words, worship Jesus, not peace. In this coming year, when we experience strife or unrest, we can minimize them by pouring into the mix of our lives as many of the raw ingredients of faith as possible; standing back and praying, we can let them and ourselves be baked in the fire of God's love. Sweet peace in increasing measure will be the result.

Growing Spiritually This Week

1. Read John 14:25–28. What sort of peace does the world give us that Jesus does not (verse 27)? What kind of peace does Jesus give that the world cannot?

2. Read John 14:25–28. Why is Jesus talking about peace with his disciples? Where is Jesus going and whom does he promise will come to help them when he is gone? What two specific things will this Helper do for the disciples—and us?

3. Read Philippians 4:4–9. What sorts of activities and thoughts are we to put into practice in order to know God's peace? When do you practice these things?

4. Slowly write the text from Philippians 4:8–9 three times in your journal. Go back and highlight each thing from the text that you are to think about (that which is "true," "gracious," etc.) in each of your three writings. What would be different in your life if you memorized and practiced these things?

The Magic of Cardboard

I finally did it, and it felt so good! After months of searching, I found the perfect present for my four-year-old son. One that made his eyes pop out, his jaw drop down, and a squeal of delight spontaneously burst from his lips... a cardboard toilet paper tube.

You see, my son's name is Ben, and because one of the greatest commercial heroes out there for young boys is "Bob the Builder," my son has completely assumed the identity of "Ben the Builder." Last year, for his fourth birthday, we pooled our finances with his grandparents and went all out to give him a toolbox full of plastic tools, a sturdy plastic tool bench, and an authentic "Bob the Builder" outfit, including bib overalls, a flannel shirt, and yellow hard hat.

Unfortunately, Ben was not satisfied with his gifts. No matter how cool he looked in his outfit, no matter how hard he pounded on his pretend bench with his plastic hammer, and no matter how hard he revved up his battery-powered drill, he couldn't actually build anything. That's when I remembered the gifts I had given his older brother when he was about the same age... cardboard in every shape and size imaginable, a few rolls of masking tape, some yarn, and a bag of rubber bands.

Now, not only is Ben more than satisfied with his new, improved set of tools, he has become a true builder. For his older sister's birthday, he built a "catch-the-button-in-the-hole" game completely on his own, using one toilet paper tube, a length of yarn, a medium-sized button, and a bunch of masking tape. They had great fun playing with it together. As Christmas approached, he was madly constructing a set of binoculars for each member of the family—again, all on his own. With the help of a book called *Look What You Can Make with Tubes*, Ben's siblings have gotten into the act, too. Toilet-paper tubes have become so popular in our house that I have caught several family members unrolling entire rolls of toilet paper, leaving the paper on the vanity next to the toilet, just so they could be the first to grab a tube they "really, really needed."

This is a good reminder that when is comes to giving great, educational gifts to kids, creativity and usability rather than expense or name brand are what really count. After getting such a gleeful response from Ben after presenting him with one small, toilet paper tube, I can't wait to see his response to all the empty wrapping-paper tubes I'm going to put under the Christmas tree this year instead of throwing them away!

I must also share that after I relayed the paper tube story to my RENEW faith-sharing group at church, a dear family in the group decided to save for us every cardboard tube that came into their house! The bulging garbage bag they gave us around Valentine's Day was full of more creative cardboard shapes than you could imagine.

Their kindness reminded me of one of the greatest—and completely free—gifts given to us at Christmas: the gift of Jesus and being a part of his Body of believers. Hebrews 10:24–25 reminds us of the eternal value of this gift by saying: "[A]nd let us consider how to stir up one another to love and good works, not neglecting to meet together, as is the habit of some, but encouraging one another, and all the more as you see the day drawing near."

Growing Spiritually This Week

1. Why do you think materialism is such an easy trap to fall into? What is the difference between giving and receiving good gifts and being materialistic?

2. Read Philippians 4:10–13. What was St. Paul's secret to being content? Think of a time you were in need. How would it have been different if you had applied St. Paul's secret?

3. Read Colossians 1:6–13. According to these verses, what is the Gospel doing? In what ways is the "cost" to for this fruitfulness being paid?

4. What nonmaterial gifts can you give to your family and church community?

A Heavenly Scent

Our oldest child called home from college the other day to say that she couldn't wait to come home for the holidays. She said that she missed walking out of her bedroom in the early morning to the aroma of freshly brewed coffee and walking in the door after a long day of high school to the smell of dinner on the table. I smiled to hear what simple things reminded her of home, and I knew exactly what she wasn't saying about eating in a cafeteria for three months straight.

Memories are deeply and somewhat mystically connected to our sense of smell. Damp leaf piles, for example, always take me back to running with my high-school cross-country team in the fall. Low tide and sunscreen smell like hot summer days at the beach and the salt marsh near our house. The smell of incense always reminds me of St. Marie Church, the extraordinarily beautiful French cathedral in New Hampshire where my husband and I were parishioners during our first five years of marriage. If ever a time machine could be invented, I believe it would be fueled by fragrances; those voiceless, invisible vapors which can transport us to another place and time with a single whiff.

There is a fantastic biblical image that makes use of our sense of smell to indicate good actions and intentions. It is "an aroma pleasing to the Lord," and it originates in the book of Leviticus in the Old Testament where God gives the nation of Israel lengthy instructions on how to properly worship him. This worship often included the offering of an animal, typically an unblemished male lamb but sometimes a dove or a pigeon, which was brought to the temple by a repentant or thankful Israelite, slain, and then burned on an altar. Cakes made of fine grains and wafers spread with oil were also acceptable, aromatic sacrifices used in worship of the One True God. To imagine the heavenly allure of all this grilling and cooking, think of catching a whiff of a neighbor's barbecue—or sitting down to a homemade Christmas dinner after eating in a cafeteria for three months!

The Bible explains, however, that it was not the aroma itself that was pleasing to the Lord. The aroma was but an analogy for the virtuous condition of the heart of the person offering the sacrifice. In fact, the Old Testament also tells us that where there is disobedient and ungodly behavior, "instead of a perfume there will be rottenness" (Isaiah 3:24).

The expression "an aroma pleasing to the Lord" is so evocative that it continued to be used in neophyte Christian communities even after Jesus' life, death, and resurrection became the perfect atonement for our sins and burnt offerings were no longer necessary. In the New Testament, for example, St. Paul thanks believers in Philippi for their financial support and other gifts by saying, "[T]he gifts you sent [are] a fragrant offering, a sacrifice acceptable and pleasing to God" (Philippians 4:18).

Having discovered how expressively the Bible uses our sense of smell, I had a kind of poetic idea for growing our faith at home over Christmas. What if each of us tried to embody our favorite holiday fragrance? What if we envisioned what we say or don't say, do or don't do, as creating an aroma as alluring as a holiday feast—an aroma pleasing to God?

All good and godly behavior would count toward embodying this fragrance, but we could take the analogy a little deeper and specifically brainstorm silent and invisible good deeds. We could bite our tongue instead of voicing negativism, judgmental opinions, or gossip. We could push the mute button on tooting our own or our children's horns, and actively listen to the stories of others instead. Invisible things we could do might be helping others without being asked (and not telling anyone about our assistance), playing Secret Santa, or spending increased quiet time in prayer. Children love codes, too, so before or during a holiday gathering we could say to each other with a whisper and a wink, "Be an aroma pleasing to the Lord." So, please don't tell my family, but I'm debating between fresh gingerbread cookies or hot buttered popcorn for my holiday fragrance, and I think I'll have to make a big batch of both before I can decide!

Growing Spiritually This Week

1. Read Leviticus 1—4. The sacrifices outlined were given to restore a person's relationship with God, to symbolize peace and fellowship with God, or to express thanksgiving to God. Who received the instructions in how to properly worship God, and for whom were

the instructions given? How many times in these four chapters does it say that the aroma of the offering was pleasing to the Lord?

2. Read John 1:29, Hebrews 9:11–28, and Hebrews 10:1–18. What does Jesus' perfect sacrifice on the cross bring about? How should we respond to Jesus' sacrifice?

3. What are some of your favorite aromas from the Advent and Christmas seasons? What memories do they spark? In what ways could your life be like a fragrance that is pleasing to the Lord?

4. If you have not done so already, share the aroma analogy of this devotion with your family. Brainstorm the holiday fragrance each of you would like to embody and begin to create a pleasing aroma.

Unwrapping the Gift of Jesus

Just a few weeks ago, a member of the weekly Bible study that my husband and I facilitate sighed in exasperation at not understanding a detail of Old Testament Scripture. "It's just so difficult to understand this stuff," he said; "it's never simple. Everything has to be learned in its original context!" We might feel the same way about obscure references to frankincense, swaddling clothes, Quirinius, or Rachel weeping during the seasons of Advent and Christmas.

Of course, our Bible study friend was right, but I happily pointed out that this was exactly why we were in a Bible study together; getting to know God better by learning to understand Scripture in context. The Catholic Church teaches that there are two ways through which we can come to know God: natural reason and supernatural revelation. An easy way to understand these two separate ways is to compare them to the two ways we can get to know our children before they are born.

When I was pregnant with our sixth child, my husband, five older children, and I got to know the newest member of our family—first, by simply watching and feeling the movement within my bulging belly;

and second, by the modern miracle of ultrasound technology. To have our older children (ages ten, eleven, thirteen, sixteen, and seventeen at the time) begin the sibling bonding process by talking to their newest sibling through the walls of my womb was utterly fantastic. And to have them at the ultrasound appointments and watch their faces light up when a hand, foot, or profile would emerge on the fuzzy screen was just pure delight!

Through the use of natural reason and supernatural (ultrasound) revelation, we developed a deeply personal relationship with Bratton Baby Number Six even before he was born. If we had not slowed down enough to observe and enjoy our baby's natural growth and development, or if we had used the miracle of ultrasound only to check for the existence of ten fingers and ten toes, it would have been a great loss. We may have gained medical information about Baby Bratton, but having information alone would not have accounted for how terribly excited we were to finally meet our little one face to face!

Of course, it is also this way in our journey to get to know God. It is a great loss if we don't allow our knowledge about God to seep from our heads to our hearts. Both natural reason and supernatural revelation are gifts God has given to enable us not just to gather data about him, but also to help us know him deeply and personally. Eager anticipation of meeting the Baby Jesus face to face at Christmas because of a preexisting, personal relationship with him—this is the essence of the liturgical season of Advent. Eager anticipation should be, in fact, the essence of our entire earthly journey toward heaven where, at long last, we will meet our God face to face, our knowledge of him will be confirmed, and our faith in his love will be rewarded.

God didn't just give these gifts of revelation to certain individuals, however. He gave them to everyone, and I'm certain that he wants us to receive them and put them to good use. To help us do this, God has also given us people who have dedicated their lives to helping us unwrap some of God's revelations about himself through the work of the Holy Spirit; among these are our priests and deacons. Like ultrasound technicians who have received special training in reading and interpreting video images produced by sound waves, our clergy and religious have received special training in reading and interpreting the Bible and Church tradition. As lay Catholics, we are no more on our own when reading and trying to understand the Bible and apply it to our lives than my family and I were on our own in trying to read and interpret the ultrasound images of our unborn baby.

To get to know Baby Jesus better this coming year, we can resolve to do a couple of things. We can pay closer attention to the priest or deacon when he unwraps a portion of Scripture during his homily at Mass. We can ask questions and seek out the help of these spiritual professionals as we learn to read the Bible and understand sacred tradition ourselves. We can pray that God will give our preachers the words we need to hear, and that he will reward their years of study and hours of preparation and practice of homilies with pews full of minds and hearts hungry for understanding.

In the same way that the ultrasound technicians made extra efforts to point out features of our unborn child to his or her already born siblings, we can request that our priests and deacons—the spiritual professionals of our diocese—make extra efforts to present homilies that point out features of our faith that are not obvious to untrained eyes.

These are the details that will make Jesus real to us, not just a plaster statue in a fake manger, a wooden mannequin on two pieces of lumber, or a storybook character from our childhood. Proverbs 29:19 states, "By mere words a servant is not disciplined, for though he understands, he will not give heed." Our priests and deacons can be visionaries that open our spiritual eyes to and translate for our spiritual ears the natural and supernatural revelation God has intended for us. They can also broaden our vision beyond the concerns that lie immediately in our paths to the more distant horizon of our true heavenly home. In the coming year, may our spiritual professionals live and minister in a manner worthy of their callings and training, and may we receive God's revelation through them in a manner worthy of true children of God.

If this happens, then we will receive our Lord in the Word and the Eucharist, and leave Mass each Sunday with a taste of what Mary and Joseph, the shepherds and magi, Simeon and Anna, and eventually the disciples experienced in the presence of the Lord: "Did not our hearts burn within us while he talked to us on the road, while he opened to us the scriptures?" (Luke 24:32).

Growing Spiritually This Week

1. What was it like to finally see your baby's face (or your niece's or nephew's face) right after they were born? How do you think you will feel when you finally see God face to face?

2. Read Psalm 19:1–6. What natural ways has God given us to understand something of what he is like? Draw a picture (or paint a word picture) of some scene from nature that reveals God's glorious existence.

3. How would you describe the priests, religious sisters and brothers, or deacons whom you know that are visionaries, showing you the ways of the Catholic faith? What is the most memorable homily or spiritual talk you have ever heard? What made it so memorable?

4. Are you ever distracted during Mass? By what? Brainstorm some ways to stay more focused.

It's a Wonderful Life

As a cold drizzle soaked the soccer fields, I huddled on the sidelines with another mom. Her only child was in third grade, like my youngest at the time, and she was sharing how she had recently reenrolled in college to finish her degree. After describing how great it was, she said sympathetically, "Well, once the kids are gone, you can get back to what you wanted to do, too."

Ouch! She didn't mean to be insensitive about my choice to focus the lion's share of my energies at home while raising our six children, but her words hurt. She implied that raising kids wasn't a valuable use of my life, so the sooner it was over the better. Her comment reminded me how undervalued mothering is in our society, even by—or maybe especially by—women themselves. Sadly, this undervaluing is felt most acutely in the "mommy wars," the civil war between women about whether or not to work while raising children, and it really clouds the more important issue of our children needing us to parent well, whether we also work outside the home or not.

As an aid in correcting this injurious outlook on mothering, I find the Christmas movie *It's a Wonderful Life* to be a splendid analogy. In this 1946 classic, we first meet George Bailey after a financial crisis has caused him to contemplate jumping off a bridge and ending it all. Now, I must admit that motherhood has, on occasion, driven me to similarly extreme thoughts, but that is not the analogy I want to explore here. No, I want to look at how George (like most modern women) grew up with big dreams. George planned to get out of his small hometown and make a difference in the great beyond somewhere. Unfortunately, events and people kept getting in George's way—events like his father's death and the stock market crash of 1929. People like his brother who never returned to help George with the family business and the local millionaire, Mr. Potter, who served as George's nemesis.

In response to these events and people, George sacrificed his big dreams little by little. In the face of each new crisis, George put himself at the service of his community rather than himself. In doing so, George acted as a type of Christ, and his community became a more loving place. Unfortunately, George didn't see the importance of his little acts of love. George believed that his life had been a waste—so much so that when the accidental loss of $8,000 put his company and family in financial and legal trouble, George entertained suicide. He thought that the life insurance money he could provide for his family by his death would be more valuable than his presence in their lives.

There are many parallels between the plight of George Bailey and that of modern mothers, but let me highlight just one. It was George's misguided perception about what was truly valuable, not his rightly guided actions, that limited his satisfaction with life. So it is for many mothers today. George, just like so many mothers, made the right life-giving choices each time he chose to invest his talents at home in Bedford Falls instead of running off to contribute somewhere more glamorous. The problem was that George couldn't see it that way. So God sent a quirky guardian angel named Clarence to show George that his life was not a waste. Clarence did this by showing George what a big difference all of his seemingly little, unimportant choices had made. At the end of the movie, George understands and begs of Clarence, "I want to live again! I want to live again!"

This Christmas season, let me be Clarence for you, just for a minute.

Thank you, Mom, for all the time, talent, and treasure you are devoting to your family. You are making a difference. Our world is a better place because of your service to your family. Thank you for all the little sacrifices—and the big ones, too. It's easy to think, like George Bailey did, that all the really fulfilling, important stuff happens outside our homes somewhere out there in the big career world. It doesn't. It's just easier to quantify out there. So the next time you feel like I did at that drizzly soccer game, sidelined in the game of life because of the life-giving choices you've made, remember this: You, just you, are more important in the life of your family than any material thing you could ever provide. Believe it, act on it, and the world will be a better place because of you.

Growing Spiritually This Week

1. What were some of your childhood dreams? Have you been able to achieve any of them? If so, what have you gained through achieving

them? If not, what have you learned in the process of either striving for them or letting them go?

2. What are your favorite parts of being a mom? Are there good parts that you never even knew to expect? What are they?

3. Has God ever sent you an "angel" to affirm and encourage you in times of questioning or despair? How might you be an "angel" for someone else?

4. Read Romans 8:28. Does this verse mean that all things are good? How can God use even bad things for his and for our good?

MIRACLES UNLIMITED

In the Gospel of John, it is written that Jesus miraculously fed five thousand men gathered on a green, windswept hill next to the Sea of Galilee. The gathering place was remote. The time was late afternoon. A chill was most likely descending on the crowd as amber sunbeams cast purple shadows across the sparkling waters of the sea. Sitting in small groups, the crowd was hungry. They must have known that there would be no place to get food when they had followed Jesus to this distant spot, but they had followed anyway. Jesus, seeing their need, had compassion and miraculously multiplied one basket of bread and fish into a feast capable of feeding the entire crowd.

When I read this story, I try to visualize what's happening. Did a new fish or loaf of bread "pop" into the basket every time an existing one was taken out, and why didn't the crowd know what was happening until it was over? I have heard interpretations that, instead of the physical multiplication of bread and fish, the "miracle" was really just the multiplication of generosity or neighborliness.

"Isn't it more reasonable," some scholars say, "that the boy who gave Jesus the five small loaves and two fish inspired the crowd to share food they already had but had been guarding for their own families?" Well, maybe, but St. John called the event a "miraculous sign," and an emotional outpouring of neighborliness has never really fit within the limits of my definition of a miracle. That is, until a modern-day miracle totally expanded my understanding of the miraculous. Let me explain.

A few years ago, my two teens and I went on a mission trip to Honduras, Central America, with the youth group from our parish. My husband and I had been praying for an opportunity like this for over three years: mission work that would immerse our teens in a foreign culture. We wanted to expand our teens' awareness of the challenges faced by our neighbors in the developing world, and we wanted them to experience the joy of being Christ's hands and feet to these neighbors. When the Honduran opportunity presented itself, we weren't sure how we were going to come up with the necessary funds (over $2,400), but following what we believed to be the Lord's leading, we signed up anyway.

We began to do fundraisers with the youth group and take on odd jobs whenever we could. Some family members also donated to our cause. Although only a few of the families on our street are Catholic, we asked all of our neighbors if they would help us raise money by giving us their redeemable cans and bottles, and they did. Then, just after New Year's Eve, we were invited to a neighborhood gathering, which is where the modern-day miracle took place. Similar to Jesus' multiplication of the loaves and fish, no one in our family was aware of the miracle until it was over.

We were seated in small groups all over our neighbor's house, feasting on an elaborate buffet, and catching up with folks when the hostess presented me with a basket of cards. I was a bit confused, until she smiled and simply said, "We think you and the kids are doing a good thing by going to Mission Honduras." At home later that night, we opened the many cards to find not only words of encouragement but generous monetary gifts that added up to the total amount we still owed for the trip!

There was no way that our neighbors could have known, but final payment for the trip was due the very next day and we still weren't sure where all of the money was going to come from. But Jesus saw, had compassion, and provided all we needed through that one basket of cards. I still believe that Jesus physically multiplied the loaves and the fish on that windswept hillside by the Sea of Galilee, but I no longer need to visualize how things "actually" happened. My neighbors' generosity showed me that miraculous signs have no limits.

Growing Spiritually This Week

1. Read John 6:1–12. Why do you think Jesus fed the crowd instead of sending them into town to find dinner? How do you envision this miracle physically happening?

2. Read John 6:22–40. How did yesterday's miracle prepare the crowd for today's teaching by Jesus? What is the disciples' response to today's teaching? What is your response?

3. Imagine that you and your family are at this hillside picnic. Draw a picture of where you would be sitting and the view of the scene from there.

4. Read John 6:41–58. Can you identify with the grumblers to whom Jesus is talking? Why or why not? Of what does Jesus assure his listeners in verses 51 and 55?

RUNNING ON EMPTY

I am unreasonably afraid of running out of gas in the car. I think it is because I learned to drive in northern Wisconsin, where running out of gas in the middle of winter could be a fatal mistake. Driving instructors told tales of fools who carelessly ventured out on old logging roads without enough gas and were never seen again.

"Freak snowstorms as early as October or as late as May are not too remote a possibility," my instructors would ominously warn. Taking their tales to heart, I developed the cautious habit of filling up my tank whenever it was down to around one-quarter full.

My habit served me well for over twenty years, but then gas prices skyrocketed and it became too expensive to keep the family van even close to completely full. Although I knew it was a necessary financial measure, driving on a nearly empty tank much of the time really stressed me out. I felt foolish and unprepared for the possibility of getting lost, being late, or running into that freak snowstorm. (Hey, October was only six weeks away!) Then, as September approached, I began to get nervous about getting our oldest kids to and from their Catholic high school thirty miles away from home.

There are parallels with the spiritual aspects of life. Am I usually tanked up on faith, or always running on empty? When a crisis comes up, do I have enough spiritual reserves to get through it? Am I as aware of my faith gauge as I am of my gas gauge? In truth, I have witnessed far more terrifying spiritual storms than hazardous snowstorms since getting my driver's license. Storms like unforgiveness demolishing relationships, materialism siphoning off family finances, and disregard for Church teaching exploding into divorce.

I can think of many good ways to stay tanked up on faith, but I'd like to focus on one: taking the Third Commandment seriously by really celebrating the Sabbath. First and foremost, this would mean getting to Mass every week, but just getting to Mass is like getting just a quarter tank of gas.

You see, keeping holy the Sabbath means more than just getting my sacraments and winning the race out of the church parking lot. A Sabbath is a "recurring period of rest and worship" based on how God rested on the seventh day after creating the world. To get spiritually tanked up, we need to stop spinning our workaday wheels once a week in order to physically rest and to refresh our relationship with God and family. This is God's plan for keeping our spiritual fuel gauges pegged on full, and Jewish and Christian cultures have lived and prospered by it for thousands of years.

Sadly, our postmodern culture seems to enjoy doing anything but observing God's plans, so the cost of really keeping holy the Sabbath is getting pretty high. The cost sometimes includes not being able to participate in sports, job opportunities, or other events that regularly take place on Sunday. Tough choices! I must tell you, however, that, time and time again, when our family has made even the smallest effort to become more of a Sabbath people, God has provided for the extra time and money we've needed during the other six days of the week. Which reminds me of how God provided for me in my anxiety about driving around with a nearly empty tank of gas.

Come September, I discovered that gas prices over at the station near our kids' high school were as much as thirty-four cents per gallon cheaper than at the one near our home! Now, by waiting to fill up near the kids' school, I can almost pay for the drive over, and I don't have to drive around on empty quite as often. Most of all, this is a tangible reminder of my need to stay fueled up on faith in order to better weather life's storms, and a promise that God will bless my efforts to get fueled up by my keeping the Sabbath.

Growing Spiritually This Week

1. We often think of the Ten Commandments as a list of killjoy "don'ts." Read Exodus 20:8–11. What was the Lord's reason for instituting the Sabbath on the seventh day? Do you think this is a good idea, independent of how it is actually implemented today? Why or why not?

2. What sorts of things can be gained by going to Mass that can fuel you for the rest of the week?

3. Imagine a perfect, godly Sabbath with your family. What does it include, beyond going to Mass?

4. Make a list of everything that keeps you from having a Sabbath and why. What could you do to eliminate at least two things on that list?

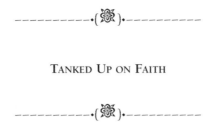

Tanked Up on Faith

In the previous devotion I wrote about the importance of keeping our spiritual fuel tanks full in order to better weather the storms of life. I touched on one way that God had planned to help us do this by asking us to regularly and really observe the third commandment, "Keep holy the Sabbath." But there are those weeks when the road from one Sunday to the next is a lot longer and bumpier than usual. Unexpected U-turns in relationships, traffic jams in projects at work or home, or bizarre detours thrown in the path of normal life can have us running on spiritual fumes before the middle of the week. Then what? How can we refuel in the middle of our always-in-overdrive daily lives?

Jesus provided a plan and a pattern for us to do this when he took the Ten Commandments and summarized them into the two greatest commandments in Mark 12:28–31:

> One of the scribes came and…asked him, "Which command-
> ment is the first of all?" Jesus answered, "The first is 'Hear, O
> Israel: the Lord our God, the Lord is one; and you shall love

the Lord your God with all your heart, and with all your soul, and with all your mind, and with all your strength.' The second is this: 'You shall love your neighbor as yourself.'"

Regularly and really keeping the Sabbath holy surely falls under the first of the greatest commandments, so this week I'd like to explore how we can stay tanked up on spiritual fuel by following the pattern of the second greatest commandment. I can think of three major ways to love neighbor and self, thereby staying tanked up on faith between Sundays: daily prayer, regular Scripture reading/study, and service to those in need.

Daily Prayer

Like the sacrifices we might need to make to truly observe the Sabbath, making time for meaningful daily prayer might cost us a little more than a quick prayer before meals. Don't forget, I'm talking about having enough faith on reserve for the demands of coworkers, in-laws, and school principals. Setting the alarm fifteen minutes earlier for uninterrupted time to pray before being swept into the day's activities might be a good place to start. (If you're reading this book, you're already on the right track, and there are also good devotional guides like *Magnificat* or *Our Daily Bread*.) Going to daily Mass and saying a rosary while commuting to work are two more ideas.

Regular Scripture Reading and Study

Regular study of Holy Scripture is the second way I'd recommend guarding against running out of spiritual gas midweek. Most parishes offer weekly Bible study groups or RENEW groups. If your parish does not, or if you can't attend for some reason, you can purchase Bible study guides through a number of good Catholic publishers.

Service to Those in Need

Loving one's neighbor does not have to be a drain on your spiritual energy level. It does not have to involve finding the time to join a group, or the money to support a service project. It's a matter of living the spiritual truth: "It is in giving that we receive." The neighbors I most regularly serve are those who live in the bedrooms just down the hall from mine. It is my service to these dependent little neighbors that both drains and refuels me as a mother. By regularly and lovingly putting myself at the service of my children (and my husband), I am teaching them to do the same for the neighbors who live down the street, over the bridge, across the country, and around the world. To receive a spiritual boost midweek, we can give love to the needy in our own homes.

Growing Spiritually This Week

1. How have you been able to maintain your daily prayer time with God? What benefits have you received from this commitment?

2. If you are working through this book in a group, what has enabled you to continue getting together? What good has come out of meeting together? Are there others you could invite to join you?

3. Who do you serve the most during the week? What is your heart attitude toward these people? What do you receive in return for your service?

4. How might we become aware of and take action on other ways to love our neighbors?

CREATIVE MEMORIES AND CRAZY MOMS

"Did you see that, Mom?" squealed my seven-year-old daughter. "Did you? Did you?"

"Yes, honey," came my distracted reply. I didn't know for sure what "that" was, but I was hoping I had actually seen it. My daughter had recently begun playing the harp, and I was in the middle of taking some pictures to send to her grandparents.

"Do you know what that's called?" she challenged me.

"Well, no," I confessed, "but maybe you could tell me."

"It's an octave!" she said triumphantly. "Wait until I show my harp teacher. She is going to be really proud."

Truthfully? I had not seen her stretch her growing fingers across eight harp strings and successfully play her first octave. I had been so engrossed in getting a picture that I hadn't even noticed if she was actually playing the instrument or not, and now I felt like a real heel.

"I am really proud of you, too," I said, putting aside my camera and focusing my attention on my satisfied little girl. "Would you play that for me again?"

The photo shoot with my junior harpist was not the first time I had fallen into the trap of valuing a photograph of an event over actually participating in the event. This particular trap is easy for me to fall into because I am the designated photographer for our family, and after attending a few heritage-building workshops, I have been inspired to be purposeful about creating and capturing our family's history as it happens. I have learned about scrapbooking, staging more spiritual birthday parties, sewing story quilts, conducting family devotions, tracing our family tree, and even celebrating patron saints' days—all really fun and creative stuff. It has been my experience, however, that it is pretty easy to focus too much attention on the planning, per-forming, and preserving of these things and not enough on the people involved.

Before we go crazy trying to create and record parties, weddings, first Communions, graduations, we need to remember that it is not these highlights of family life but rather the ordinary, loving exchanges between family members that make up the real and rich tapestry of a family's heritage. Using a little poetic license, I tweaked a Scripture verse to remind me to focus as much on loving people and living in the moment as I do on planning events and recording those moments. 1 Corinthians 13:1–7, 13 (recently and creatively revised version):

> If I speak in the tongues of photographers and scrapbookers, but have not love nor time to play with my children because ("Look, kid, can't you see I'm trying to get this photo album done?") I am only a resounding gong or a clanging cymbal. If I have the gift of making story quilts and can fathom all embroidery stitches, and all weights of cotton fabric, and if I have a tone of voice that can make kids sit still during wed-dings and family devotions, but have not love, I am nothing.

If I give all the energy I possess to volunteering and organizing the family reunion and surrender my body to late-night cupcake making, but have not love, I gain nothing. Love is patient; love is kind. It does not envy its neighbor's camcorder; it does not boast of finishing this year's scrapbook; it is not proud of knowing where each child's baptism candle is. Love is not rude to those standing between my camera and the ballet stage, it is not easily angered over ruined birthday parties, and it keeps no record of whose child did the ruining.... And now these three I still remain in need of before the party begins: not more balloons, a bigger hall, or a fancier dress, but faith, hope, and love, and the greatest of these is love."

Growing Spiritually This Week

1. Read 1 Corinthians 13:1–13. As you read, substitute the word "Jesus" into the text every time the word "love" is written. In what ways does this word change affect how you understand the love of Jesus and how you should be showing love to others?

2. What are some practical examples of how we can keep our activities from running (or ruining) our relationships? How can constant distraction work against our good intentions?

3. Sometimes we forget that we alone are not responsible for all things! Read 1 Corinthians 12:12–30. According to these verses, how can we keep a healthy balance between showing and recording our love for our family?

4. What is your favorite keepsake from your childhood? Why is it so special? Have you thanked the person(s) who created it for you?

Prayer, Our High-Speed Connection to Heaven

We live in the communication age. I'm sure this is nothing new to anyone who has progressively added cable TV, high-speed Internet charges, and cell phone text messaging to their monthly bills. Instant communication. Knowledge at our fingertips. It has become the accepted way of things.

With instant communication so readily available, however, I wonder if we might have put our connection to heaven on hold, or even hung up on God completely. Perhaps, without even intending to, we've filled with idle chatter and instant messaging the little bits of time we previously took to personally connect with God through prayer. Driving in the car. Walking the dog. The last few minutes before fading off to sleep.

Here's a test: The last time you had fifteen minutes to spare did you (1) call a friend, (2) hop online, (3) flip on the tube, (4) plug in your iPod, or (5) find a quiet place to pray? Of course, I'm setting you up here, but really, can you remember the last time you stole away to pray? Stole away to be with the Lord because you just had to tell him something, or because you just needed to be in his presence?

In the Old Testament (1 Kings 19:9–13), the prophet Elijah is searching for the presence of the Lord God Almighty. Along the way, he experiences a lot of loud, forceful things: a wind so powerful that it tore the mountains apart, an earthquake, and a great fire. It was not until there came "a still small voice," however, that Elijah knew he was in the presence of the Almighty.

The voice of the Lord came to Elijah in a whisper, not a shout. Perhaps a good Lenten sacrifice this year, one in keeping with our day and age, might be to turn down the technological clamor a little bit in order to listen for the gentle whisper of the Lord. In other words, when we feel the urge to be connected, we could turn to prayer instead of to our cells phones or computers.

When praying to God from the heart, the letters in the word "ACTS" can serve as a helpful guide.

Following the pattern of the Lord's Prayer, it goes like this:

Adore God: Begin by telling God how wonderful he is. Adoring God puts our hearts in right relationship with him and naturally leads us to the next letter.

Contrition: Acknowledge our sins and telling God that we are sorry for them. Sin is the big and the little ways we've turned our backs on God and fallen short of the wonderful ways Jesus taught us to live and to love.

Thanksgiving: After we've repented of our sins and received forgiveness, we will want to thank God for all the graces and blessings he has showered upon us.

Supplication: We end our time of personal prayer by asking for help, healing, and guidance from God for ourselves and others, especially those who have asked us to pray for them.

When I was teaching my kids how to pray from their hearts after receiving holy Communion, I came up with a shortened version. It's easier to remember because the first words are all verbs—the "acts" we perform while praying.

Applaud God's Greatness

Call on God's Mercy

Tell God Thanks

Say, "Help"

A parting thought on acting on the call to spend more time with God in prayer is to mention Eucharistic Adoration. Even a few minutes sitting in the presence of the Blessed Sacrament is a beautiful experience of listening for God. Leave the cell phone in the car; you won't need it to hear God whispering how glad he is to see you.

Growing Spiritually This Week

1. In what setting(s) do you find it easiest to pray? What is it about these places that creates an environment of prayer?

2. Read 1 Kings 19:7–13. Where was Elijah and why? Why do you think God was not in the wind, the earthquake, or the fire, but in the still small voice? How can you create more time to hear God's gentle whisper?

3. Concentrate on the first two letters of the acronym ACTS. Why do we show adoration for God? How do we show it? Why and how can we call on his mercy?

4. Concentrate on the second two letters of the acronyms ACTS. How can we tell God thank you? Where do you need God's help?

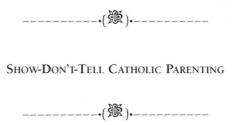

SHOW-DON'T-TELL CATHOLIC PARENTING

I am a strong believer in the principle that children learn more from their parents' actions than from their words. It's a principle that I call "show-don't-tell Catholic parenting." Last year, I had an experience that drove home the truth of this principle. On the way to a high-school football game, I had to drive through an unfamiliar region of southern Massachusetts. With directions in hand, I approached a busy five-way intersection and took a guess as to which lane I should be in to go straight. I guessed incorrectly and ended up in a left-turn-only lane. I stayed in the wrong lane with my blinker on signaling a right turn and readied myself to jump the green light in order to still go straight. I accomplished this illegal maneuver successfully and endured only a few outraged honks.

Truthfully, it was such a minor happening in the big picture of my life that I forgot about it as soon as it was over. Then, one day about six months later, I was driving a carpool when one of the teens in the car mentioned seeing me at that football game.

"Oh," I said to this teenaged friend, "I don't remember seeing you there."

"No," this friend answered, "I drove in another friend's car, but we got lost because of you."

"What?" I quipped back, not sure how this could be true.

"Well," this teen began, "the friend who gave me a ride did not have very good directions, but on the way there I saw your car and told her to follow you because you would know the way. But when we got to that big intersection—you remember, the one with the five different streets—well, we had to turn left when you cut off those cars and went straight. It was pretty dark by the time we found our way back to the game."

"We remember that!" my own children chimed in as bells started ringing in my head, and I humbly said,

"Ah, yes. That intersection. Now I remember."

I hadn't meant to mislead these teens. I was more than fifty miles from home and not even aware that they were following me. But following they were, and they got lost because of me. After apologizing to this friend, three principles of show-don't-tell Catholic parenting were embossed on my mind:

- Even when we don't know it, our children—and perhaps their friends—are watching us.

- Even if we are miles away from home, alone, or unseen, there is no such thing as taking a vacation from being Catholic. (Not long after the carpool conversation, I hit the confessional about my illegal maneuver and causing the teens to get lost.)

- Most importantly, and much more significant than showing our children the way to a football game, is showing them the way to our Father in heaven. We can't just talk about it; we must do it, too!

In John 14:6–9, Jesus tells his disciples about the way to the Father:

> "I am the way, and the truth, and the life; no one comes to the Father, but by me. If you had known me, you would have known my Father also; henceforth you know him and have seen him." Like Jesus with his disciples, it is through us that our children first come to know what God is like.

Without a doubt, show-don't-tell Catholic parenting is an enormous undertaking. We need God's help to do it. With God's assistance, we can begin to see that how we talk to one another, what we watch on TV or at the movies, how we use the Internet, and who we associate with when we are not at home all affect who we are and how clearly or how faintly God's face is seen through our own. With God's help, we must strive to be people of integrity. We must strive to behave in the same way when we are away from our families as we do when we are with them. And, yes, even when we are driving, we must show ourselves to be truly Catholic.

Growing Spiritually This Week

1. Who were your role models when you were growing up? What was it about them that you liked? Did they always measure up to your admiration?

2. Read John 14:6–21. According to these verses, can we know what God is like? Why is Jesus our perfect role model?

3. In what situations are you are tempted to "cut corners" in living an authentic Catholic life? How could you do a better job of modeling the Catholic life to your family? To others observing your life?

4. What help in being godly role models does Jesus promise you in John 14:15–18? What are some of the ways you can stay connected to Jesus as you try to be a better role model?

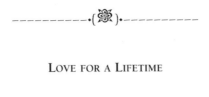

LOVE FOR A LIFETIME

It seems to me that romantic love is by nature spontaneous. Thinking back to when my husband and I were dating, I remember my stomach leaping into my throat every time the phone rang. What should I say if it was him? I remember when his hand brushing mine caused my heart to skip a beat.

Following the normal cycle of getting married, starting careers, and having children, the impulsive nature of our love has matured. What was once a high-spirited maple key, swirling down from the sky, has been planted and grown into a steadfast tree. This steady, "love is a choice" kind of love has given us the strength to weather temporary activity whirlwinds, and longer term seasons of stress as a couple. I am grateful that we now share both kinds of love, because I believe God designed marriage to be both passionate and practical. The trick is to continue romancing even after the wedding bells have stopped pealing and routine has set in.

My husband and I had the privilege of being taught the importance of this in premarital counseling by several Catholic couples that had been married for twenty-plus years. These couples talked openly about the importance of a healthy sexual relationship, so, with St. Valentine's Day around the corner, I'd like to share some key bits of their wisdom.

The first key they taught us was to learn and practice the art of Natural Family Planning (NFP). As a way to naturally regulate child-bearing, NFP is one of the most misunderstood and underutilized gems of Catholic teaching. Among couples that practice NFP, however, there is not only an incredibly low divorce rate, but also an incredibly high rate of satisfaction within marriage. I did a little research and found that only 2 percent of couples that practice NFP get divorced, as compared to the national divorce rate of 50 percent. I also found that 89 percent of the women who practice NFP seem to share a deeper intimacy with their spouses than women who do not practice NFP (www.familyplanning.net/index-home.html).

The long and short of NFP is that it is much more than a natural method of birth control. Practiced faithfully, it is a marriage tool that facilitates better communication, more self-giving, and, yes, possibly more children. Whether a couple desires to have or to postpone having a child, they use the same awareness of the wife's ovulation cycle to decide when to share the marital embrace. Of course, periodic abstinence in marriage may not sound like it helps spontaneity, but a monthly agreed-upon recess from sex throws spouses back into the dating years, helps them not to take sex for granted, and reminds them to cultivate nonsexual ways of expressing their love. Clearly these are not theological reasons to practice NFP, but our premarital counselors were not theologians. They were just calling it as they saw it and lived it: obedience to Church teachings about NFP had the positive side effects of heaping multiple blessings on their marriages.

The second and third keys from our premarital counselors were to pray together daily and to continue dating each other. They taught us that, by praying together, we would not only feel the relief of lifting our burdens to God, but also the companionship of sharing our burdens with each other. We have made it a priority to continue dating weekly, or at least trying to, and it has kept our romance alive. Over time, our daily prayer time together has also become a mini date. Listening to each other's prayers not only helps us keep in touch with daily happenings but with each other's souls.

With regard to love that was promised for a lifetime, it takes intentionality to preserve spontaneity, especially amid the complexity of family life. By practicing NFP, praying together daily, and scheduling dates, romance gives way to routine, which carves out occasions for romance, which gives way to routine...so that, like tree rings in a giant maple, the spontaneous and the steady natures of marriage go 'round and 'round, allowing love to grow stronger and stronger, year after year.

Growing Spiritually This Week

1. The practice of NFP is one of the most valuable gems of Catholic teaching, yet it is still very much a diamond in the rough when it comes to widespread knowledge and use. Divert from your regular devotions today and log on to www.ccli.org. Spend fifteen minutes browsing the site, following links to questions you may have about this system of planning family size.

2. How might both you and your husband's being more observant of your monthly cycle of fertility be helpful to your marriage? How could agreed upon periods of abstinence alternated with agreed

upon periods of intimacy as outlined in NFP teachings be good for your marriage?

3. In what ways could you pray with your husband? How could your relationship be improved if you prayed together more regularly?

4. Recall your courtship. What activities brought you closer together? What are some ways that you could recover some fun and romance with your spouse?

----------•(❀)•----------

Planting Seeds of Faith at Home:
Reflections for Lent and Easter

----------•(❀)•----------

Not So Fast

As March approaches, the talk in our house turns to what we will give up for Lent. Chocolate, coffee, and candy bars make up the three Cs of fasting for me because they are the little luxuries of life that I love the most. The Lent I gave up coffee was as grueling an experience as trying to plant tulip bulbs in frozen February ground, but God taught me something that year that helps me even now.

Every Monday afternoon of that school, year my oldest child attended CCD about twenty minutes from home. My usual routine was to go to a nearby coffee shop with the four younger kids (ages two, four, five, and seven at the time) and let them pass that hour playing with straws and cups. I would savor my coffee, read the paper, and hope the kids wouldn't make too much of a mess. I could have engaged them a bit more, I know, but by four o'clock in the afternoon, my creative juices had been bled dry.

The first Monday of that particular Lent happened to be a cold, drizzly day, so I was eager for my cup of comfort. Except it was Lent.

"Oh, man, as if the day wasn't miserable enough," I objected. "What does fasting really do except ruin my day?" I grumbled to heaven.

"Who is going to die if I just go anyway and have a cup of tea, or even the coffee I want?"

I was on the verge of going, but I felt the Lord asking me to give up the whole coffee experience in favor of doing something more kid-oriented. I look back at the experience now and just laugh. What a spoiled little child I was being about not getting what I wanted that day!

Following the promptings of the Holy Spirit, I did give up the whole coffee shop routine that first Monday of Lent and headed to a small children's museum nearby instead. The kids had a blast and were completely entertained without an ounce of input from me. It turned out to be a better situation all around. Why hadn't I thought of it earlier in the year? Oh, yeah, because I had long ago filled that time slot my own way. In retrospect, I can see that God took my grumbling as a question. He taught me that no one was going to die if I broke my fast, but if I kept it, it just might allow for something better to happen.

We don't fast during Lent in order to avoid punishment, to strut our spiritual stuff, or to coerce God into doing something for us he otherwise wouldn't do. We fast in order to loosen our grip on the luxuries and indulgences of this world or, maybe more importantly, to loosen the grip they have on us. We fast in order to cleanse ourselves of things that have usurped the place that God is supposed to occupy in our lives. Here are some ideas to consider when choosing your fast this Lent:

- Try fasting as a family. Soda. Condiments. TV. Slippers. Fasting as a family gives everyone the chance to bond and support each another, so pick something creative, even funny, for the whole clan—and stick to it.

- Do something positive. This is a good idea for young kids who don't really have too much control over what they eat, when they watch TV, or the like. For kids of First Communion age and older, though, I think there is more merit to giving something up. Self-sacrifice for a good cause is among the most important disciplines to teach and model for children as they mature in their Catholic faith.

- While we are fasting, we can't forget to pray. Fasting and prayer go together like Adam and Eve. Prayer helps us focus on the event for which we are fasting (Easter in this case) instead of on the fasting itself.

Let's look for creative ways to use this Lent to remove one thing from our lives and then wait expectantly to see what God can teach us through this simple sacrifice.

Growing Spiritually This Week

1. Read Matthew 6:16–18. Jesus gives a "how-to" lesson on fasting. How can you improve your fasting based on this instruction?

2. Read Hebrews 13:15–16. What types of sacrifices are offered here? In order to offer up these sacrifices, from what must we fast?

3. While reading Matthew 4:1–11 and Psalm 35:11–14, record who fasted and why they fasted.

4. What will you give up this Lent, and for what purpose?

Sunlight and Lent

As a photographer by profession and by nature, I am constantly aware of sunlight. Watching sunlight move through the day, arranging itself around objects and landscapes in ever-changing ways, is a constant source of joy and hope for me. It is, perhaps, for this reason that enduring the winter months when the sun gets up late and goes to bed early can be a challenge. As early as four o'clock in the afternoon, while there is still much to be done in my day, the beauty of twilight is snuffed out by the cover of night.

There are other things about winter that make it challenging for the natural photographer in me as well. The winter landscape lacks color. Trees clothed in the delicate greens of spring and summer and in the brilliant reds, oranges, and yellows of autumn are stripped to a uniform brown in winter. Barren branches provide good studies in contrast and pattern, but all in all they are not nearly as spectacular as branches plump with leaves, flowers, and fruits.

In order to compensate for the loss of sunlight and color in my world, I have trained myself to look for evidence of spring's return amid the winter months. Did you know, for example, that as early as January, leaf buds appear on tree branches? More amazing yet, rivers of sap begin to flow in barren tree branches around the end of February. I know this is true because since I was a kid I have tapped maple trees, collected the sap, and boiled it down to the amber sweet goodness of maple syrup.

Even today, I carry on this tradition with my own kids, filling the dry, winter air in the house with sweet-smelling clouds of maple mist. Looking for tree buds and making maple syrup reminds me that even though nature appears to be dead in the middle of winter, it is, in fact, just waiting—like I am—for the return of the sun before springing to life again.

It is during these waning weeks of winter and maple sugaring that Catholics are called into the liturgical season of Lent. Frankly, I am of a split mind about the timing of this. On one hand, I always want to say, "But I've given up sunlight and color for months now. What greater sacrifice can I offer up than to be joyful even without the beauty of sunlight to catch my eye? Lent is really just too much to bear on the heels of winter."

On the other hand, I think that Lent couldn't come during a better time of year. The coinciding of Lent with days of ever-increasing sunlight provides us with an ideal chance to spiritually join with nature in anticipating the return of a different type of light at Easter: the Light of the World, Jesus Christ. By stripping from our lives some of the things that naturally give us pleasure, Lenten sacrifices help us see through the temporal happiness of the world to Jesus, who hung on the barren, wooden cross for our sins and by this sacrifice became our ultimate source of joy, hope, and life.

As we enter into the season of Lent this year, let us offer up our sacrifices, but—using nature as our guide—let us also train ourselves to look closely for signs of new, spiritual life even in the most hopeless corners of our world. These signs may be as small as leaf buds in January—signs like a standing argument between two family members that doesn't ignite because one member exercises self-control and pinches the fuse. These signs may even be as invisible as sap running through trees in February—signs like an increasing personal desire to read and understand Scripture, or an interior yearning to participate in the Mass more often. They are small or invisible, but they are still real.

Pretty much impossible to photograph, these are the signs of new life for which we should eagerly look this Lent. They are evidence of the Light of the World shining into our souls and preparing us for an Easter season of life flourishing with the gifts and the fruit of the Holy Spirit.

Growing Spiritually This Week

1. Read John 1:1–9. Who is John calling "the light" in these verses? How are life and "the light" connected in the natural world? How are they connected in the spiritual world?

2. Read John 3:19–21. In what ways would it be better to live in the light rather than in the darkness? Why then are we told in these verses that some would prefer to live in the darkness?

3. Read John 9:1–11. How does the healing of the blind man illustrate who Jesus is? Can we experience spiritual blindness?

4. Read Matthew 5:13–16. If Jesus is already the light, how can we also be the light? In what ways can we let our light shine instead of hiding it under a bushel?

Through fasting, almsgiving, and prayer, the forty days of Lent provide us with special opportunities to express solidarity with those who struggle to meet their basic human needs. With this seasonal opportunity in mind, the next four reflections focus on a mission trip I took to Honduras, in Central America. While I recognize that not all families will be able to go to a foreign land, we all have opportunities in our own families and local communities to serve the physically and spiritually needy, as well as to support the work of those ministering abroad. If you will be using these four devotions to grow in your faith as a group, make an extra effort to stick to the reflection questions as they are written. You will be covering distinct aspects of Catholic mission work each week.

Mission Endurance... I Mean Honduras

I spent the February school vacation living out of a carry-on bag, taking cold showers, digging ditches, killing scorpions and centipedes, and chaperoning fifteen teenagers. Sound like a nightmare? It wasn't. It was a little taste of heaven on earth called Mission Honduras, and I had the extreme privilege of serving in this mission with our church youth group.

Sponsored by my parish, our group was made up of fifteen teens and ten adults. As a group, we spent eight months prior to the trip trying to understand and prepare for our journey, but all we could really do was pray, plan, and pack, and then pack, plan, and pray some more. During our time of preparation, parishioners overwhelmed us with their generous support. Trip costs for the kids were defrayed by participation in multiple parish fundraisers. Over twenty-five hundred pounds of medical and school supplies were donated for us to bring for the schools, orphanages, clinics, and housing projects that make up Mission Honduras. As final plans were laid and suitcases packed, we were feeling successful and proud of all we would be bringing to the needy, but we were still unsure what exactly what this experience was going to be like.

It wasn't until a week before our departure, when the founder of Mission Honduras, Fr. Emil Cook, came to celebrate Mass, that we began to have an inkling of the transformations that God would be doing in our midst. In his homily, Fr. Cook urged us to understand that, as Catholic missionaries, our primary purpose was not merely to bring humanitarian aid. It was to be Christ. It was to show love and concern by reaching out to the needy in their place of need. Being a missionary, according to Fr. Emil, was less about outwardly changing the world than about allowing love to transform the inner world of our souls.

With Fr. Emil's words as a compass, we finally gathered our bags and headed south. Somewhere between our 3:00 AM departure and our 2:00 AM return nine days later, we were transformed as individuals and as a group. What brought about those transformations is hard to put into words, but where we began our trip with name tags, hellos, and handshakes, we returned with nicknames, *holas*, and hugs.

During our time in Honduras, I watched shy teens come out of themselves and embrace shoeless Honduran toddlers. I breathed in the hot Honduran dust as we labored to dig a foundation trench for part of the mission's high-school compound. I heard laughter and joy spilling out of simple, cinderblock homes in the Center for Abandoned Women and Children—homes completely devoid of modern conveniences like hot running water, washing machines, telephones, and microwaves. I savored fried tortillas and spicy refried beans as our group gathered nightly in the volunteer house for physical and spiritual nourishment.

Among our teens, I witnessed creativity, cooperation, openness, humility, and a willingness to do even the hardest of jobs without complaining. I beheld love in action. I saw the next generation of Catholics alive and breathing, and I was filled with a sense of great hope for our Church.

While on our mission trip I was given a glimpse of frontier-style faith, and it was refreshingly pared down and simple. It was about love of Christ and of neighbor. The experience honed my vision for what I still need to teach my own kids about the Catholic faith, and it left me hungry to share that vision with other families. Over the next three reflections, I'd like to explore the importance of our being a missionary Church, one that is alive and kicking, proactive and growing. I promise not to share too many "survivor" stories about killing scorpions or chaperoning teenagers. In truth, however, it is much easier to live with both than you might expect when you first meet them.

Growing Spiritually This Week

1. Read John 20:19–23 and Mark 16:15–19. What mission did Jesus give the disciples? Who did he send to give them help?

2. When you think of missionaries, what images and feelings come to mind? Do they jibe with the Scripture passages of Question 1?

3. If a calling to the sisterhood had been your primary vocation, what work would you do? Where and with whom would you do it? Why?

4. Spend time in prayer today for all missionaries, especially ones you know personally. Pray that God would meet their needs and confirm their work.

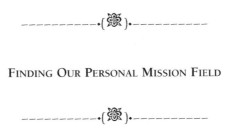

Finding Our Personal Mission Field

At morning Mass on Ash Wednesday, we sang a closing hymn called "The Summons" by John L. Bell. The lyrics go like this:

> Will you come and follow me if I but call your name?
> Will you go where you don't know and never be the same?
> Will you let my love be shown? Will you let my name be
>   known,
> Will you let my life be grown in you and you in me?
>
> Will you leave yourself behind if I but call your name?
> Will you care for cruel and kind and never be the same?
> Will you risk the hostile stare should your life attract or scare?
> Will you let me answer prayer in you and you in me?

It was the perfect song to give confidence to those of us who were timid about wearing an ashen cross on our forehead for the rest of the day. I had a doctor's appointment right after Mass, and I have to admit that I was feeling embarrassed about walking in with a large smudge of charcoal on my face. Never mind that my three youngest kids would be walking in right behind me with the same smudges on their faces!

Beyond encouraging me to "risk the hostile stare" or just look silly for the sake of my faith, the lyrics brought back fresh memories of our trip to Mission Honduras. It had only been four days since we returned, and the people I had meet there were still close to my heart and in my daily thoughts. While singing "The Summons," I felt like shouting, "Yes, Lord! I'll risk all that and more for you. Just send me back to Honduras." Yet, here I was in the States, feeling fainthearted about wearing a little ashen cross on my forehead for the day.

I had no problem sticking out like a Caucasian sore thumb in Central America, hugging orphans, wearing my "Mission Honduras" t-shirt everywhere, and firing up my rusty Spanish in an attempt to communicate with the locals. I didn't feel a bit embarrassed about sticking out by being Catholic down there, so why was I so apprehensive about wearing my faith on my sleeve—or on my forehead—now that I was back home? Perhaps it was because down there I was not just Heidi, I was a *missionary*. Up here, I am just-your-average-Heidi, and sticking out is something I'd rather not do, even for my faith. The inconsistency of my own heart convicted me, and bittersweet tears filled my eyes as we finished the song.

Where is the mission field, and how do we know if we are called by God to go there? The answers to these questions lie at the core of our Catholic faith. When we confess in the Nicene Creed that we believe in "one, holy, catholic, and apostolic Church," we are affirming that our Church is "missionary of her very nature" (*CCC*, #866–870). We are saying "yes" to the missionary mandate given by Jesus in Matthew

28:19, "Go therefore and make disciples of all nations." The funny thing about applying that mandate is that "here" is a place, too.

Here, in my hometown, is where I found myself on Ash Wednesday, and the doctor's office was where God was calling me "to go and never be the same." The receptionist definitely did a double take and suppressed a giggle. The doctor couldn't look me in the eye, and I'm sure that he and the nurse exchanged raised eyebrows when they switched places in the examination room, but there I was, being a missionary with my own kids, no special t-shirt, and speaking my native tongue. As Catholics, our mission field encompasses every doctor's office, classroom, and living room in every corner of the globe, because no matter where we live, each of us is close to God's heart and in his thoughts every day.

Growing Spiritually This Week

1. Read James 2:14–25. What is the right relationship between faith and deeds? According to James, what does the term "love in action" mean?

2. What does the term "love in action" mean for your life in this present season of family life?

3. Think of a person you know personally who exhibits the mind and actions of a missionary within the vocation of spouse and parent. Describe this person and what you think enables them to live this way.

4. Sketch a drawing of or write a paragraph about yourself engaged in the work of a parent missionary.

Todos con Juntos

Kneeling on a red tile floor in front of the Blessed Sacrament, I heard a gecko chirp. I opened my eyes to search for it and saw Bert the cat silently pad by on his way to the altar. In utter amazement, I watched as Bert sat down behind the altar table and joined us in adoration of the Eucharist by reverently gazing at the monstrance for about ten minutes. It was such an extraordinary experience that I had the urge to pinch myself to see if I was dreaming, but I knew I was not.

Between rural Honduras, where Bert lives, and suburban Cape Cod, where I live, there are many differences. The way animals and people live more closely with each other and their land is one of those differences. A good example of this interconnected way of living is the high-school compound at Mission Honduras where our youth group labored to dig a trench. In the twenty yards between the high-school building and the girls' boardinghouse, chickens roam freely. If you walk another twenty yards, you've already passed the modest school building and are in danger of falling into a pond full of tilapia fish. Circle around the small pond and through a stand of banana palms, and you will come to the first of three large cornfields. Tucked behind the rows of corn and some ornamental trees is the mission's chapel. Students who are blessed enough to attend this high school spend their mornings in class and chapel and their afternoons tending to the animals and crops, the sources of all their food. The Spanish phrase to describe this type of communal living is *todos con juntos*— "with everything all together."

That phrase, *todos con juntos*, best describes the way I felt during our mission experience. Back home, my life is much more compartmentalized: work, worship, school, and social commitments are locked in an almost constant tug of war. But in Honduras, for one short week every facet of my being—body, mind, and spirit—was working in unison and focused on the single goal of being Christ to the needy. It made me feel whole and fully alive, like fresh-squeezed orange juice instead of Tang.

I had purchased a few Honduran souvenirs, but as we packed our bags to leave the mission it was this sense of wholeness that I most wanted to bring home and give to my family. Without moving to a mission, here are some ways that I think it is possible for us as American families to live more *todos con juntos*:

On a daily basis

• Learn to care for animals; pets, wild birds, frogs, and fish are all great options.

• Connect with each other through daily prayer. Pray for each other's needs at work, school, and church.

• Eat dinner together as a family. Do not allow TV, phone, or bickering to intrude.

On a weekly basis

- Do household chores together.
- Attend church as a family. Make Sunday special by spending more playtime together.
- Establish a family night. Do something all together: cook dinner, play board games, or take a walk.

On a monthly basis

- Pick a good book and read it out loud together.
- Hold family concerts and plays. Sing together.
- Commit to a family service project.

On a seasonal or yearly basis

- Plant, grow, pick, or catch some food together and prepare and eat it as a family.
- Be active together. Adventures like camping, boating, or picnicking build wonderful bonds and memories.
- Celebrate big when it comes to Church holidays and liturgical seasons of the year like Advent and Lent.

If we as parents will purposefully tend to the life of our family unit by regularly doing these types of activities, I believe our families will be more cohesive, more *todos con juntos*, even without the chirping geckos, praying cats, or swaying banana palms.

Growing Spiritually This Week

1. Describe or draw pictures of activities that unite all members of your family.

2. Entry number 2206 from the *Catechism of the Catholic Church* (*CCC*) calls the family "a privileged community called to achieve a 'sharing of thought and common deliberation by spouses as well as their eager cooperation as parents in the children's upbringing.'" Rewrite this definition in your own words.

3. Recognizing that most often our homes are our mission houses, how could we go further than sharing joint activities to building shared thought, common deliberation, and eager cooperation with our spouse and children as outlined in *CCC* #2206?

4. Read James 1:27. In what ways can our desires for a good and godly family life and our actual family members be in conflict? Extrapolate from the verse in James to show how we should care for others and ourselves when our expectations and experiences of family do not line up.

GIVING FROM THE HEART

My heart is so fickle. I came home from our mission trip to Honduras deeply convicted about increasing our financial support of missionary and charitable organizations, but I haven't done it yet. Specifically, I wanted to give more to the needy in the developing world. I saw how much we in America have compared with those in Honduras, and it touched my heart. My husband was completely amenable to the idea of boosting our giving, but once we dove into the budget and looked at the needs of our own family, I got cold feet. I became afraid. To cut items from our budget in order to give more money away just didn't look reasonable or even possible. Mind you, we do not live extravagantly, but with only one breadwinner in the family and trying to provide the children with a Catholic education either by homeschooling or paying tuition at a Catholic high school, our income is totally spoken for before it even hits the bank account. If an appliance breaks, a car needs repair, or a child gets sick, we are in big trouble. A dear friend and Irish-born nun, Sr. Angela, used to call it "livin' on a bit of a shoestring," and how right she was. But still, in comparison to the people I had just met in Honduras, we are at least the king and queen of the shoestring factory.

Of course, Lent is a time set apart not only to fast and pray but also to give alms. So, timing-wise, the past five weeks turned out to be the perfect season for me to wrestle with my fears of giving so much that my own family would suffer. We have always supported our local parish, specific missionaries, and certain Catholic institutions. We think it is our responsibility to do so, but personally, I have ducked and dodged Bl. Mother Teresa's advice to "Give until it hurts, and smile." With a smile or not, I do not like to hurt.

Turning to the Bible and Church teachings, I began to look into the topic of Christian giving. First I found that Christian giving is not something one does out of financial surplus, but rather off the top, before calculating living expenses. Ouch. Secondly, from the time of the Old Testament, the biblical standard of giving has been a tithe of 10 percent of a family's gross income, measured in grain, animals, or dollars. That amounts to four hours of wages from a forty-hour workweek. Double ouch. Thirdly, I consulted the new papal encyclical, *Deus Caritas Est* ("God Is Love"). In it, Pope Benedict XVI wrote the following: "For the Church, charity is not a kind of welfare activity which could equally well be left to others, but is a part of her very nature, an indispensable expression of her very being" and "within the community of believers there can never be room for a poverty that denies anyone what is needed for a dignified life." I couldn't duck or dodge any longer. At the Stations of the Cross one Friday afternoon, I looked up from all my external researching and internal wrestling and caught sight of the crucifix. Jesus did not stop giving because it hurt. Jesus didn't give what was reasonable. Jesus didn't calculate his giving to exactly 10 percent and then say, "There, I've done my part." He gave it all. And it hurt.

Oh, dear Lord, I would hand over my entire shoestring kingdom for a heart like yours. For a heart that could hold on to the images of the heartbreaking tin-and-cardboard homes I saw with my own two eyes and the sickly Honduran baby I held in my own two arms. For a heart that could embrace and not let go of the simple truth that everything that I think is mine is really a gift from you.

From the struggle of this Lent and in the sorrow of this Good Friday, I ask for an Easter sunrise where I could truly give you my heart. And, more than that, please, grant me a glorious springtime where I won't take it back again. But, please, at least give me the strength to start with what Bl. Mother Teresa said and to "Give until it hurts, and smile."

Growing Spiritually This Week

1. Read James 5:1–6. James is not condemning wealth but the love of wealth. What is the heart attitude he wants us to have toward money? What difference might it make in your life if your heart attitude about giving was closer to James' attitude?

2. How do you regularly support the Catholic Church and her many charitable programs? What could you do to increase your support? What or who would you like to support more?

3. Consider being more financially creative than just writing a check. Are there needy ministries, groups, or individuals for whom you could purchase and donate something? List them and what they might need.

4. Reread the quote in the devotional from Pope Benedict in *Deus Caritas Est*. Read the entire encyclical if you can. Why do you think charity can't be separated from who we are as Catholic Christians? What might happen to the Church if we tried to leave all charitable giving to the government or other groups?

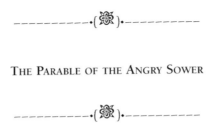

The Parable of the Angry Sower

"What happened in here?" I demanded to know, rushing into my daughters' room after hearing a loud crash, followed by an even louder scream.

"I didn't know it was open," wailed my five-year-old son, shrinking down beside his seven-year-old sister who was crouched on the floor.

"You didn't know what was open?" I began, before noticing the birdseed. It was scattered absolutely everywhere. Three pounds of birdseed on unmade beds, over cluttered desks, in toy boxes, throughout laundry baskets, inside open dresser drawers—everywhere! I stood there in shock, trying to fathom the impossible odds of ever cleaning it all up. The tragic tale presented to me for how this happened was something about "not sharing," and "not giving my blanket back," and "no, it was my blanket." None of which seemed to be connected with the scattered seed, which was the thing I was ready to cry about.

"Enough about the blanket!" I yelled, totally losing my cool. "What's with all the birdseed?"

"He threw the jar off the dresser when I wouldn't share my blanket," my seven-year-old answered, unaware of having revealed her true part in the drama. It was my turn to sink to the floor. At that moment, I wished with all my heart that the jar had been closed too, or that my son had thrown something far less messy. It would have made my job of dishing out appropriate consequences so much easier.

The event was a good word picture for the widely scattered effects of personal sin. Rarely do we realize just how far reaching the consequences of sin can be, or how hard it may be to clean the consequences up. Even little sins can have vast consequences—gossip, for example, or not telling the whole truth, or fudging the numbers…just a little bit.

Like my five-year-old son screaming, "But I didn't know it was open," sometimes we see the visible consequences of our sins and feel remorse for them. But how often do we look deeper and try to find the "real deal" or the cause of our action that may not be so visible? In my son's case, the real deal was throwing (anything) out of anger when his sister did not share her blanket. (It was her blanket, by the way, and her root sin was that of enjoying torturing her little brother by not sharing with him.)

Strewn birdseed was the immediate result of my kids' misbehavior. Having to apologize and help clean up the birdseed were their immediate consequences. But learning not to throw things at all and to share things more freely were their real deals. And my real deal? The reason I got so angry and was throwing angry words around like birdseed? First of all, it's because, although we often hate to admit it, parents are human, too. Secondly, at the time this incident went down, we were expecting company for dinner in about fifteen minutes.

Fortunately for all of us, the consequences of God's grace extend farther than those of our sin, the broadcasting of God's forgiveness farther than that of our transgressions. Grace, by the name of Jesus, reaches down from heaven and offers to cleanse every corner of every repentant heart—kids' hearts and parents' hearts, too.

The humorous and humbling image that sprang to my mind as I grappled with what to do in the next fifteen minutes before our guests arrived was that of Jesus stretching down from heaven with a really, really powerful vacuum hose. After cleansing my heart of the sins of overreacting and yelling, he handed me the hose and said, "Now, you have at it. Tell the kids you're sorry and start cleaning up the harsh words you've thrown all over before they spill out of this room and totally mess up the evening you've planned with your friends." No longer angry sowers, we exchanged apologies, crunched our way out of the room, locked the door, and made a pact not to open it until our friends had gone home.

Growing Spiritually This Week

1. Read Ephesians 4:29–32. List what we are told to do and not to do as believers in Christ.

2. Journal about a time when a seemingly small sin—gossip, slander, lying—had a larger, negative impact on your life. What could have been done instead?

3. Read Colossians 3 and 4. As you read, continue your list from Question 1.

4. Consider at least two separate situations in your life where the temptation to sin is very strong. What can you do to either avoid those situations or to act as Scripture commands in them?

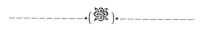

Getting on Track and Bearing Good Fruit

Is it just me, or does modern family life seem to have been thrown into the backseat of a fast-moving minivan? Parents and kids alike are living as though life were a drag race, speeding past historical markers and scenic vistas with the pedal to the metal. Forget swinging in the backyard. It's hurry up, get 'em out of diapers, and off to college so we can retire to Florida. The trouble is, if we apply the race analogy to raising a family, I think the journey is going to be more like the Indy 500 than a drag race.

The Bible gives us at least two analogies of what we can expect life to be like. One is that of running a race, as found in Hebrews 12:1–2: "...Let us also lay aside every weight, and the sin that clings so closely, and let us run with perseverance the race that is set before us, looking to Jesus the pioneer and perfecter of our faith..." Reading these verses, I sense that instead of setting out at top speed, we are being told to set a sustainable pace, to become less frantic and more focused about life in order not to burn out in the first mile.

The second image of what life will be like is that of tending a vineyard (or a garden). Zechariah 8:12 is an especially beautiful verse about this analogy: "For there shall be a sowing of peace; the vine shall yield its fruit, and the ground shall give its increase, and the heavens shall give their dew." Of the two biblical images—running a race or tending a garden—I think the gardening analogy paints a more realistic picture of family life. That is, I think it is more accurate to expect that raising a child will be more like a ripening of fruit and less like a crossing of a finish line.

Visualizing parenting as something that will be done in seasons—planting, tending, and harvesting—frees us to enjoy the process. Although our focus is still toward the end (harvest time), when we bear fruit, our joy is in seeing the seedlings (our children) mature and blossom and bear fruit of their own. Jesus speaks to this ripening process in the Gospel of John 15:8, 16: "By this my Father is glorified, that you bear much fruit, and so prove to be my disciples.... You did not choose me, but I chose you and appointed you that you should go and bear fruit and that your fruit should abide."

In order to visualize parenthood in this way, I carry with me an image of my children as seedlings planted indoors in starter trays in March. Cold winds still chill the air outside and the ground remains frozen as the lime-green shoots poke up through the cups of black dirt and strain toward the sun in the window. The time is not yet right to transplant them outside our home. But the one who planted the seeds continues to nurture the shoots through April, until the warmth of May or even June has come and the now-sturdy sprouts are ready for the garden, safe from the dangers of late frosts.

Raising sturdy, confident kids takes time and patience, but days will turn into years. Our children will not always be toddlers, underfoot and needing our constant attention as seedlings in March. Neither will they always be teenagers hanging around and growing as rapidly and in every direction as bean sprouts in July. What joy it would be to slow down and put family life back in the driver's seat. What peace it would bring to park the car in the driveway for a bit and tend to the particular season our families are in right now. Florida isn't going anywhere soon.

The beautiful truth in all of these analogies is that parenting is not a competition. Childhood is not something to be raced through. Family life is not measured in the numbers of mile markers blown by and sights checked off, but in milestones commemorated and picnics enjoyed. Let's get back on track (or step off the track) and remember that family life is about love nurtured, joy planted and grown, and faith ripened, harvested, and shared.

Growing Spiritually This Week

1. Read Zechariah 8:12. In what season(s) of family life are you? Tilling the soil? Planting? Tending the shoots? Weeding? Harvesting? Feasting? Leaving fallow?

2. Visualize your family as a garden. What sort of "fruit" (or plants) are your children? Draw a picture of your children in your garden.

3. Read John 15:1–17. This is an image for growing spiritual fruit. Who is the vine? The branch? The gardener? Who or what are the fruit? What must happen for good fruit to be borne?

4. List the good fruit you have seen and now see in your family life.

Housework and Heaven's Work

Know what I love most about housework? Getting it done! Know what I love least about housework? It's never done! Call me odd, or Type A, or whatever you want, but I like to clean and organize. Once a week, on Saturday morning, I try to persuade the family to see housework my way. I cheer them on with statements like, "Housework teaches teamwork. Housework builds character. Housework improves your health!" Well, OK, maybe I'm a bit grumpier than that with those unfortunate offspring of mine who try to sleep in, but at least I refrain from using the bullhorn until after eight o'clock.

A while back, there was this fantastic Saturday when we actually checked everything off the "to-do" list. It felt like we had won Olympic gold. Driving home from kids' sports events and jobs that evening, I was relaxed, ready to make some pizzas, and eager to enjoy a family movie. As I moseyed into the house, however, there squatted one of our cats, using a basket of clean laundry as a litter box! That was a topper— an eye-popping act of unspeakable insolence. What spiritual lesson was I supposed to learn from such absurdity as the cat's relieving itself in my clean laundry? I pulled out the bullhorn immediately.

When our children were babies, wise souls used to cajole me, "Let the house go. Your babies won't stay little forever, you know."

"Oh, yeah?" I'd mutter under my breath as I kept cleaning. "And just which fairy godmother do you think is going to fly in and tidy up this place with a flick of her wand?" Letting things go was a surefire guarantee that a neighbor would drop by and cock an eyebrow at the mess, that I'd lose an important bill, or maybe even lose a kid amidst the chaos. Truthfully, if my house was undone, I was undone.

Obviously, with a household of six children and upwards of twelve pets at any one time, I needed to either adjust my expectations or put in for a vocational reassignment. My adjustment happened one day through a friend who, of course, stopped by in the middle of one of "those" days. As I madly tried to explain away the disaster, my friend simply turned me around to look at the children. A couple of them were at the table painting. Two were building mazes for our guinea pigs in the living room out of couch cushions and Legos. Another child had a friend over and was baking cookies. As if I had just been given a new pair of glasses, I saw what my friend saw: creativity, learning, play, and that people were more valuable than cleanliness and order. That night I was inspired to create a kind of life slogan to frame and hang on my wall. I wrote:

Our Home Is a Theater Stage,
Not a Museum Display.

Like a theater production, life is…well…lively! Unlike a museum display, life includes people that don't always fit together nicely and events that cannot always be showcased neatly. My slogan reminds me that housework is not an end in itself. The purpose of keeping an orderly home is to help us focus on the people we live with, not to showcase either the home or the people. Trust me, though; I haven't given up my desire for order and cleanliness entirely. Doing so would make me as ludicrous as our cat. What I have embraced is the fact that life at our house is often like a theater production in full swing, and cleanliness and order cannot always have center stage.

Other people may have the opposite reaction to housework. They may run from it like the plague, but to ignore the care of our homes isn't the answer either. Housework is important because it prepares the stage for the physical, spiritual, and intellectual development of everyone who lives there. In its proper priority, housework is heaven's work. I read of a grandmother who put it like this: "Keep a house that is neither so messy nor so tidy as to make guests uncomfortable." Sounds to me like another inspired slogan to hang on my wall.

Growing Spiritually This Week

1. Read Luke 10:38–42. Who was the principle owner of the home Jesus was visiting? What exactly did she want from Mary? Why? From Jesus? Why would he tell her to lay aside her concerns?

2. Parents—even moms—have the right to things like sleep, eating in peace, a clean house, and going to Mass. Sometimes, however, God asks us to lay down these rights for the greater, common good. In doing this, we must realize that these things still remain ours. Which does it feel like to you more often, that these rights are taken from you, or that you voluntarily lay them down for the greater good? Why?

3. Draw a bundle of twigs being held by two hands. Label each twig with something you have the right to do or have as a human being. Draw a second pile of twigs lying on a table. Label these twigs with the things you volunteer to give up for a time for the greater good of your family.

4. What is your heart attitude toward the "twigs" you've given up? What can you do to make your attitude closer to what Jesus advises Martha in Luke 10:38–42?

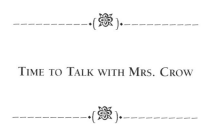

Time to Talk with Mrs. Crow

It is a long-awaited spring morning after a damp New England winter. I have cautiously turned off the heat in the house and opened the windows just a crack. As I sit on the couch with my seven-year-old daughter as she practices her math flash cards, it seems as if we can see and hear nature waking up through the open window. Crocuses dot the lawn. A crow fills the air with loud cries. I imagine the crow is a mommy, noisily building her nest.

Suddenly, a raspy shriek comes from right under our window. My daughter and I jump out of our seats, flash cards flying to the ground. I try to suppress a giggle, but as my daughter looks at me with wide eyes, I burst into laughter.

From the throat of her five-year-old brother, who is playing just outside the open window, we hear another series of child-sized caws. Having no idea that anyone can hear him, my son has taken up a conversation with Mrs. Crow! We peak out the window and watch him alternate between digging in the dirt and talking with Mrs. Crow. The whole morning is the fresh reminder of what I love about being a mom: just being with the kids.

The morning's experience is an answer to prayer, because other signs of spring have been coming to my attention too; however, these other signs have brought me anxiety rather than joy. Flyers for kids' summer camps have recently begun appearing in my mailbox.

Many of us moms have discussed the possibilities of sending a couple kids to one camp or another. We have stopped short of signing up, however, because of some combination of scheduling conflicts and finances. It's a combination worth talking about in light of coming to grips with the fact that, for most families (certainly for ours), "you can't have it all," even though "having it all" is exactly what pop culture screams we are all absolutely entitled to and must have.

Up until this morning, I had been really wrestling with the choice. Feeling the pressure to conform to society's expectations with unusual strength this past winter, I had begun to believe that if we didn't provide our kids with organized science, sports, art, and/or music camps in the summer, they would fall behind, be left out, and lose out on all the learning they'd absolutely need to succeed in tomorrow's world. I had begun to think that it wasn't enough to work hard at keeping expenses down so we could keep one parent at home. What would the kids have to put on their resumes when applying for fifth grade honor society?

But this morning's events quieted my anxiety and the noise of pop culture. In the few and precious summers of childhood, I think it best to give my kids time to talk with Mrs. Crow—time to explore the backyard with their sibling and neighbors, time to develop interests without pressure, time to connect with the God of the universe by smelling the roses and gazing at the summer stars, time off from the activity merry-go-round. Why? Because, to me, giving the family time to regenerate and reconnect with one another in the summer seems to be in keeping with the gift God gives us of a weekly Sabbath, just on a larger time scale.

OK, OK—I'm not completely immune to societal pressure. For those who ask, I may cave just a little bit and call our family time together "Free-range Summer Camp." (I wonder if the honor society would call for an explanation of camp events?) Honestly, I'm happy with our choice, even though it's a choice not to attempt to have it all. I really believe in the value of family time, and that family time can't happen if we're always cooped up and scheduled up. And now, because her voice has so influenced our summer "un-plans," I think I will go outside and join my son in talking with Mrs. Crow.

Growing Spiritually This Week

1. Read James 5:7–9. What "moods" are conveyed in these verses? What is the chief virtue encouraged here?

2. List the activities, events, holidays, and seasons you treasure most with your family.

3. Describe or draw a picture of your family engaged in one or two of the activities you listed in Question 2.

4. List the names of your children. List the opportunities you'd like each to have. Put a check by those that are incompatible with the treasured family activities you listed in Question 2. Could the activities you've checked be done in a family-friendly way? If so, how? If not, cross them out and trust God to provide for your child's growth and development in his own way and in his own timing.

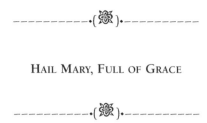

Hail Mary, Full of Grace

As parents, we stopped asking questions about certain things long ago. "Why is the sky blue?" for example, or "Why do cats have whiskers?" We enjoy hearing a child ask these sorts of questions, however, because they remind us to wonder at the beauty of God's creation. As an adult, I have developed the habit of bringing my childlike questions to God, our Heavenly Father. I bring my questions to him with the attitude of the father of the demon-possessed boy in Mark 9 who exclaimed, "I believe; help my unbelief!" My questions always begin, "God, I believe what you have revealed though Scripture and tradition, but I was wondering…". I can almost see God kneel down and pat me on the head when I tug on his heavenly robes in this way.

"My dear Heidi, it's just not as complex as you think," he replies with a grin.

"Yes, Lord, I know," I respond, "but I'm still not getting it. Could you give me a visual aid?"

About five years ago, I began asking God to help me understand a mystery about Mary. I couldn't grasp that if sin is what condemns us to hell, and Mary never sinned, then why did she need Jesus as her savior?

Years went by with no insight provided. Then, while the kids and I were preparing lunch recently, I had a revelation.

My ten-year-old had just put a pot of water on the stove to boil spaghetti when she asked how high she should turn the heat. I replied without thinking, "You can turn it on as high as you would like; water doesn't burn." Sitting nearby, my eight-year-old thought this very curious and asked, "Why not?"

"Well," I explained, "because water evaporates instead of burning." As those words slipped out of my mouth, my son's question became a word picture to answer my question about why Mary needed a savior, too. I'll explain in nonscientific terms the insight God gave me.

Water is a not like regular "stuff." Stuff burns. Water does not. In the same way we throw water on stuff to stop it from burning, it is the presence of water inside of stuff that can prevent it from burning in the first place. An example of the first situation would be throwing dry spaghetti noodles onto a hot fire. In a few seconds the dehydrated pasta would burst into flames. To save the spaghetti from burning, we would have to pour water on it. An example of the second situation would be putting spaghetti sauce in a hot pan. Due to the presence of water already in the sauce, it wouldn't burn as quickly as the noodles did. Preexisting water in the sauce would prevent it from burning. In both situations, however, it is the water that saves the stuff from burning.

If we go back and substitute "Jesus" for "water" in the previous paragraph, we see that our condition at conception is much like that of the dry pasta. We are born "dehydrated"—without the grace of God due to original sin. In order to be saved, we have to have the waters of baptism or the grace of God poured over us and into our lives. Mary, on the other hand, was born fully hydrated—or "full of grace," as the angel called her at the Annunciation. Mary's condition was more like that of the spaghetti sauce. In both situations, however, it is Jesus that saves both us and Mary.

I know that mystery is a part of the faith life, but I believe that God delights in the deeper questions and wonderings of his earthly children. I further believe that he wants to help us understand our faith more fully and will therefore answer our questions, even if it takes years. If there is something you've been wondering about, I encourage you to give a little tug and say, "Father, I believe, but I was just wondering…".

Growing Spiritually This Week

1. Read Mark 9:14–29. Put yourself in the place of the boy's father. Would you have been as honest with Jesus in the face of your son's great need and Jesus' promise? When was the last time your honestly shared your doubts with God? What happened?

2. Read Luke 16:19–31. Reread verses 27–31. What do you think prevented Lazarus and his brothers from believing what they already knew about their faith from hearing stories about Moses and the prophets? What prevents you from belief in the teachings of Scripture and the Church?

3. Read Matthew 13:10–17. What separates those who see and believe from those who see and don't believe?

4. Make a list of doubts you have regarding God, Jesus, the Holy Spirit, the Bible, the Catholic teachings, or anything regarding your faith life. Offer your doubts up to God, believing that he will help you overcome your unbelief.

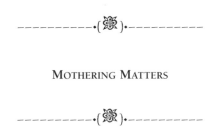

Mothering Matters

Recently we had the supreme pleasure of being a foster home for a litter of stray kittens and their mother. Six fuzzy little bundles of gray, black, and brown stripes, the kittens were only four weeks old and still nursing when a friend asked if we could take care of them. She didn't have to twist my arm very hard. Maybe only my pinky finger.

We cleared space in our mudroom for a good-sized cat bed, multiple water dishes, and two litter boxes. We purchased a few kitten toys, but they attracted the kittens' attention only briefly. What these bundles of joy really liked to do was to chase their mother's tail day in and day out. Mommy cat took it well, but I noticed that she would occasionally creep away from her young 'uns and curl up by herself in a laundry basket full of beach towels stored on a shelf. Watching her do this, I smiled to myself, remembering the many bleary-eyed years I spent nursing babies, then handing them off to my husband and crawling back into bed to get a little more sleep.

One morning, about a week into caring for the kittens, we came into the mudroom to find one of the kittens missing. We began frantically searching for this gray-and-white fuzzball amid the cat toys, coats, boots, and canned goods also housed in our mudroom. Before long we found her, not in danger but snuggled up with her mother in the laundry basket. I smiled again at the similarity between this mommy cat, her kittens, and my own mothering experiences.

When the kids were of preschool age, I would try to wake up before they did in order to "sneak in" some prayer time before the day began. Without fail, the kids would wake up earlier, too—and find me. If I cleared a corner in the house to do a project, it would become their new favorite hangout. I learned very quickly that a playroom full of new toys simply couldn't hold a candle to Mommy's lap.

As a society at large, it is the beauty of this mother-child bond that we celebrate on Mother's Day. As family units, we celebrate the specific women in our lives who have looked long and hard at their many choices and, by saying "yes" to motherhood, have let love and life win out. In the grand orchestra of family life, mothers are the conductors. In the construction of hearth and home, mothers are the master builders. Against that which would corrupt innocence, mothers are soldiers on the home front, the guardians and shepherdesses of childhood. To fledgling teens, climbing out on the limbs of self-sufficiency, mothers are the safety nets. To young adults, navigating the waters of autonomy, mothers are the lighthouses. Mothering is an act of great courage and hope. Mothering is a personal investment in the future. Should we ever doubt the importance or influence of mothering, we need look no further than to Mary, the Mother of our Lord, whose simple *fiat* ushered in the possibility of redemption for the entire human race.

Tragically, from the litter of kittens we fostered, all but one died from distemper. Amazingly, the striped fuzzball that survived was the one that had sought and found her mother in the laundry basket. After two months of veterinary care, we adopted this kitten. Incredibly, one of the first things she did when we brought her home again was to race to the mudroom and jump up into her mother's laundry basket. I swallowed a lump in my throat as we watched her sniff around the beach towels, curl up in a ball, and go to sleep. Although mommy cat was gone, her mothering had left a lasting impression. Mothering matters. Mothering makes a lasting difference. Happy Mother's Day to all my mothering colleagues out there, and thank you for letting love and life win out. I appreciate you.

Growing Spiritually This Week

1. Make a list of the impressions about life that your mother or the primary female influence in your life left on you. These impressions will most likely be positive and negative if you are honest, so list some of both.

2. How have you (and how are you currently) letting love and life win out for your children, thereby leaving them a legacy of faith?

3. In what ways do you see motherhood as an act of courage and hope? An act of shepherding and guiding? An act of building for a better tomorrow?

4. Who has been your greatest role model in mothering? Your greatest support? In what ways are you like or unlike these role models?

TAKE SMALL BITES AND KEEP ON CHEWING

In the midst of raising a family, it is easy to get weighed down with the basics of childcare and lose the joy of watching our children grow and mature. My kids are bright and full of life, as I know every parent's children are, and I want to do my best to launch them into this world. The problem is that I often feel like I'm not making any headway. My primary *modus operandi* is to go flat out and just get the job done. Nothing makes me happier than crossing something off my "to-do" list, which is probably why I find it so demoralizing to wake up to the same "to dos" on my mothering list each morning.

"Why does everyone have to eat again today? Didn't I just feed them yesterday? Didn't I just clean that floor and fold those socks? When do I get to move on to the big things, like teaching them to be good grown-ups? I'm trying to raise a family here—what's with the messy little details?" Anyone with children can relate, I'm sure. But I have hope that was given to me by some giant Cecropia moth caterpillars.

Early one August, my husband brought home about forty of these caterpillars, and everyone was eager to watch them change from caterpillar to cocoon to moth. Each tiny, black fellow was about the thickness and half the length of a straight pin. Over the next several weeks, our new pets grew 1,000 percent, turned bright green, and grew rainbow-colored spikes. Way cool.

Unfortunately, soon after my husband brought these creatures home, he went to sea on a research cruise, the kids grew tired of the project, and the task of keeping our unusual pets alive fell to me. So, not wanting yet another repetitive chore, I stuffed their two-and-a-half gallon tank so full of wild cherry leaves (their only food source) that you couldn't even see the caterpillars. At first, the food supply lasted about three days. One morning, however, I came downstairs to see that the tank I had packed with leaves just the night before was completely empty. I did not have time for this. Thinking I could outwit the little buggers, I moved them all into a ten-gallon tank and stuffed it full of leaves. The next morning, I woke up to find those leaves completely eaten. I split the group into two twenty-gallon tanks, and guess what? The next morning, all those leaves were gone too! Looking at those puffy green pain-in-the-necks, which were now approaching the size of meaty hot dogs, I realized that my *modus operandi* wasn't working. I had lost my joy.

So where was the hope I promised to deliver? Just what did our caterpillars teach me about hanging on to the joy of family life? Two things: Take small bites and keep on chewing. I kept trying to finish feeding our caterpillars. They just kept on chewing. I wanted to get the job done, just like I want to get the laundry, the shopping, and, oh yeah, especially the cleaning done. But our caterpillars knew that really big jobs don't get done that way. Our caterpillars showed me that I couldn't possibly launch my children into this world in one big burst of energy. That's because I can't possible stuff enough love into them to last for more than about one day. I must press on in doing all the little repetitive tasks needed to create a loving home for them and trust that in the end these things will add up to a successful launch.

Take small bites and keep on chewing. It's the same advice Jesus gives when he instructs us to pray that God will "give us this day our daily bread." Notice that Jesus does not tell us to pray that God will heap on us, all at one time, all we'll ever need to live our lives, but only enough for one day, like manna in the desert. Take small bites and keep on chewing. It's my new mode of operation, and I can feel the joy coming back already.

Growing Spiritually This Week

1. Read Matthew 6:5–15. What sorts of things constitute our daily bread? Organize these things into your physical, intellectual, psychological, emotional, and spiritual provisions.

2. How can you allow God to provide your daily bread for the span of one day? Draw a picture of yourself receiving some portion of your daily bread from God the Father.

3. List some ways you can physically and intellectually feed your children during the span of one day.

4. List some ways you can spiritually and emotionally feed your children during the span of one day.

---------(✿)---------

Tending to the Faith at Home:
Reflections for Ordinary Time in Summer

---------(✿)---------

Like a Mighty Wind

With the celebration of Pentecost, we pause to consider the third person of the Holy Trinity, the Holy Spirit. The first person of the Trinity is God the Father. Known as the Creator of the universe, he is awesome. And then there is Jesus the Son, the second person of the Trinity. Jesus, by his death and resurrection, paid the price for all the sins of all humankind for all time. That makes Jesus pretty awesome, too. The problem is that sometimes the Father and the Son seem just a little too awesome, a little too big for me to wrap my arms around. What I long for is the God who knows me personally, and that is where God the Holy Spirit makes his entrance.

In the New Testament, the Holy Spirit is depicted as a dove, a flame, and the wind. I can most easily relate to the Holy Spirit by envisioning him as the wind: "When the day of Pentecost had come, they were all together in one place. And suddenly a sound came from heaven like the rush of a mighty wind, and it filled all the house where they were sitting" (Acts 2:1–2). I can relate to the wind because my husband, John, taught me how to windsurf back when we were dating. If there was "a mighty wind" when we got off work in the evening, we would race to the lake of our northern Wisconsin childhoods, hoist our sails, and get on our boards. On windless summer evenings, we'd rush to the same lake and water ski or sometimes canoe with the loons through glassy calm waters. On any given evening, it was the wind that told us what to do with our free time together.

Have you ever paused to listen to the wind? If you have a kite, a mighty wind might tell you to head to an open field. A calmer current of air might tell you to wait for another day. If you have a sailboat, a mighty wind might beckon you to lash everything to the deck and head to the open sea. A gentle breeze might tell you to bring a grill on board and enjoy a tranquil, sunset meal.

While learning how to windsurf, I spent a lot of time doing headlong somersaults into the water. John, who had learned earlier and more quickly, spent a lot of time sailing patient circles around me. Learning to sense and align ourselves with the movement of the Holy Spirit is a similarly personal journey, but it is one that Scripture invites each of us to take. Every day, the same Scripture readings are proclaimed in every Catholic church throughout the world. I envision those readings as a wind emanating from the pulpit and blowing across the congregation. When we are told by Jesus to forgive seventy times seven, it is like a mighty wind. The strength of that particular Scripture should cause each of us to grab our hats and hang onto our pews, as the Holy Spirit reveals specifically to whom we need to offer forgiveness. At another Mass, we may hear the comforting message that Jesus heals the broken-hearted. These words arrive like a gentle breeze, delicately opening the door of personal healing for wounds we've hidden deep within. It is according to each person's situation in life that the same wind delivers a different message.

John 3:8 proclaims: "The wind blows where it chooses, and you hear the sound of it, but you do not know where it comes from or where it goes. So it is with everyone who is born of the Spirit." To receive God's personal direction for our lives, we must keep watch for the wind that is the Holy Spirit. If we will but turn our faces toward that Spirit-filled wind, we will know whether to raise or lower our sails, fly our kites, or paddle our canoes. We will feel the touch of the Holy Spirit and know that, no matter how awesome or big he is, our Triune God knows and loves each of us personally.

Growing Spiritually This Week

1. Read Acts 2:1–4. The Holy Spirit is clearly real; he was both seen and felt by the believers gathered at Pentecost. What can we learn about the Holy Spirit from these descriptions of him?

2. Has God revealed (or would you like God to reveal) himself to you in such recognizable ways? Describe your experience(s) of God's presence in your life.

3. Read John 3:8. How is our need to stay in tune with the Holy Spirit illustrated in this passage? How would your life be different if you were more in tune with movement of the Holy Spirit?

4. How would you use the Scripture you've read to describe the Holy Spirit to a young child? To a teenager?

Prayer: A Window to Heaven

We have three "indoor" cats. I am chuckling just now at the largest one, an orange tabby. She is napping on a window seat in our house while a squirrel raids the birdfeeders only inches beyond her through the clear glass. I chuckle because I know this cat, Blondie, would go insane if she knew her nemesis were so close.

Yesterday Blondie was clawing at the same window, yowling and trying desperately to penetrate its transparent, hard nothingness to get at that twitching squirrel tail. By some fluke of lighting and acoustics, the wild creatures outside this particular window can neither see nor hear through the clear glass back into our house. Therefore, much to Blondie's dismay, none of the squirrels that frequent our birdfeeders have ever been affected by her, no matter what kind of ruckus she raises. Domestic cat and untamed squirrel, while living at the same time and in nearly the same place, exist in two, completely separate realities: the indoors and the outdoors.

We, too, have a window into another world, and that world is heaven. However, between the earthbound reality in which we live and the divine reality where our heavenly Father lives, I think the lighting and acoustic tricks are exactly reversed. Although we know by faith that heaven exists, we can neither see nor hear from it clearly with our own eyes and ears. Nevertheless, and also in direct contrast to my cat and the squirrels, God has given us the great gift of being able to affect the activity of heaven through prayer.

Prayer is a multifaceted activity. At its very essence, prayer is the movement of our soul toward God in response to his blessings. We adore God through prayer. We petition God, intercede for others, thank God, and praise him. In each of these activities, we are asking to share in God's goodness, searching for the coming of his kingdom here on earth, and hoping for all things to be well. Prayer is the foundation of our personal relationship with God—and therefore the foundation of our family's faith life. Personal prayer is not just important; it is vital to the Christian way of life.

Of course, understanding what prayer is and actually doing it are two different things. I have to confess that I have sometimes behaved like Blondie is behaving right now and taken a little catnap during Mass. And during that catnap, Christ was present in the Eucharist right in front of me! At other times, I have prayed diligently for specific needs, but felt like my prayer went completely unheard. In fact, I felt pretty much like Blondie looked yesterday—like I was petitioning, clawing, and yowling out to God and getting absolutely no response. This is when I have to lean on faith and believe that God does hear and will answer every prayer even though I'm not seeing any tangible results. St. Paul tells us in 1 Corinthians 13:12, "For now we see in a mirror dimly, but then face to face. Now I know in part; then I shall understand fully, even as I have been fully understood."

The trick to effective prayer, I think, is to seek out those occasions that naturally draw our souls toward God, just like Blondie is drawn to the window each day by the sight of those squirrels. Because we are unique individuals, these occasions will be different for each of us: holding a newborn baby, smelling a Christmas candle, saying the rosary, feeling an ocean breeze, seeing a child's bedroom, clean and tidy when you didn't even tell them to do it. Morning sunlight kaleido-scoping through a stained glass window awakens within my soul the desire to pray. The smell of a deep pine forest and hearing my husband really laugh cause the same response.

What is it for you? What makes your soul aware of our one, true, unseen God and makes you yearn to communicate with him? Whatever it is, do it as often as you are able. Unlike my indoor cat and the outdoor squirrels whose worlds will never coincide, in some mys-tical way love is able to transcend its natural boundaries, and heaven and earth embrace when we pray.

Growing Spiritually This Week

1. Why might you not give detailed descriptions to young children of where you are going on a car trip? Read 1 Corinthians 13:12. Why do you think God has given us the gift of prayer instead of a clear window into heaven?

2. Read 1 Timothy 2:1–8. What four types of prayer are mentioned in these verses? For whom are we supposed to offer these prayers? For whom could you pray for today?

3. What have you done in the past to develop quality prayer time in your daily life? What could you do now to improve your daily prayer life?

4. Meditate on God's many blessings in your life. Thank God for these blessings, and notice any changes in your desire to draw even closer to him in this process of prayer.

A Fatherly Kind of Love

I happened across a quote the other day that captures perfectly my experiences of fatherhood. The quote is from a small book entitled *Radical Hospitality: Benedict's Way of Love* by Father Daniel Homan and Lonni Collins Pratt. In describing a friend of theirs named Joe, the authors said, "He knew not the name of intimacy but the meaning." Joe, they said, "probably could not have articulated the meaning of hospitality, but he knew how to pour you another cup of coffee. You would leave Joe's company feeling taller, stronger, and more human."

Like Joe, there are some great dads out there who are better at demonstrating their love than verbalizing it. One reason for this, perhaps, is that dads have faith in their kids' potential. Dads assume their kids can do it, no matter what "it" happens to be. Because of this, dads are comfortable trusting their children with things like hammers and nails, two-wheeled bikes, and lawn mowers a lot sooner than moms are. Dads give extremely high pushes on tire swings to show their affection. Dads are more apt to wrestle than to cuddle. Dads understand the need for superlatives like climbing the highest, racing the fastest, and eating the most.

While I was in high school, my dad helped me train for the fall cross-country season by taking long runs with me in the summer when he came home from work. One of the things I remember best about those runs is that he always beat me. I treasure that memory because my father showed me that I wasn't a child anymore by not sandbagging. He knew that in order for me to realize my potential as a runner, I had to be pushed, not coddled. Like the authors who had spent time with Joe, I felt "taller, stronger, and more human" after running with my dad because I knew that if I came even a little closer to his finishing time, it was a genuine accomplishment.

Like my dad, my husband trusts in our kids' potential. He let our oldest jump off the diving board way before I was comfortable even letting her swim in the deep end of the pool. I don't think he even thought twice about it. She asked if she could try; he said, "Sure," treaded water in front of the diving board, counted to three with her, and "Kersplash!"—down she jumped. When her wide-eyed, smiling face bobbed up from under the waves, she was "taller, stronger, and more human."

One of the most poignant biblical stories about fatherhood is the parable of the prodigal son found in Luke 15:11–32. The father's lavish acceptance of his wayward son upon his return is the highlight of the story, but I always wonder what possessed the father to let the son go in the first place. Where was the mother crying out, "Are you crazy, Papa? You can't give him his inheritance early. That boy's got holes in his pockets and wild ideas in his head, and you know it!" But the prodigal's father also knew that no amount of coddling was going to turn his boy into a man. By letting him go, the prodigal's father gave his son the chance to grow "taller, stronger, and more human," and because of it, the son became all those things—and a great deal more humble to boot.

God, our heavenly Father, has taken the same risk by trusting us, his children, with free will. John 3:16 says, "For God so loved the world that he gave his only son, that whoever believes in him should not perish but have eternal life." That verse shows us how much God believes in us. Rather than lowering the bar or taking away the possibility of perishing, God has made heaven a choice and given us the chance to grow "taller, stronger, and more human" by allowing us to choose for ourselves. That's a distinctively fatherly kind of love, and on this Father's Day, I thank my father, my husband, and all the great fathers out there for the times they have embodied such love.

Growing Spiritually This Week

1. Did you feel "taller, stronger, and more human" in the company of your father? Did you have any other male role models that helped you grow up (teachers, priests, or coaches)?

2. Read Luke 15:11–32. By requesting an early inheritance, the prodigal son was actually rejecting his father, saying in effect that he wished his father were dead. What, then, is extraordinary about the son's return?

3. The story of the prodigal son is actually an analogy for God's unconditional, fatherly love for us. What is keeping you from running to God the Father and becoming reunited with him? What would God want you to do with these things?

4. How could you help your children have an even better relationship with their father? In what ways could this improve their image of God the Father?

Father Knows Best

Two-year-olds are not the only ones who dislike hearing the word "no." I'm forty years old, and I still prefer a nice, accommodating "yes!" Of course, the problem is that many times "no" is a more loving answer than any of us, young or old, want to admit. For example, the other day I was all set to slide into the perfect parking spot in front of the soccer field when another car sneaked into the spot by parking in the wrong direction.

Needless to say, I wasn't impressed. But I shrugged, parked at the far end of the soccer field, and went to play tetherball with my son while waiting for his practice to begin. While we were playing, the sneaky car left without our noticing. As my son's practice was about to begin, we heard a loud screech and turned to see a tan car careen toward the soccer field, cross the place I had wanted to park, and smash into the fence. Oh, man! No one was hurt in the accident, but the out-of-control car was totaled. Had I parked where I had wanted to park, our van would have been a goner. Thank you, Father God, that I didn't get what I wanted!

Another time that "no" worked out for the best was when we upgraded our septic system. It never occurred to us that the excavator was not going to replace the topsoil he removed when installing the leach field. When the last backhoe pulled out of the driveway, however, we were left with about a quarter acre of sand and gravel instead of a grassy front lawn. When all was said and done, we actually saved money by boxing off an eight hundred-square-foot area and creating a sand volleyball court instead of having to replace the entire area with new topsoil and grass. Family and neighborhood volleyball games have been a favorite activity ever since! Thank you, Father God, that the excavator said, "No, replacing the topsoil was not part of our contract."

In my parenting experience, "no" isn't any easier to say than it is to hear. It is a natural, parenting urge to want to provide our children with every advantage, every possible good thing. The truth is, however, that we can't give our children everything, and ironically, giving them every good thing isn't best for them, anyway. It's a bit like arranging a bouquet of flowers. The number, size, and color of the blossoms we choose not to put in an arrangement are as important to the final look as the number, size, and color of the blossoms we do put in. What we don't give our children is just as valuable as what we do give them in determining who they will become.

St. Paul tells us in 2 Corinthians 12:7–9, "And to keep me from being too elated by the abundance of revelations, a thorn was given me in the flesh, a messenger of Satan, to harass me, to keep me from being too elated. Three times I besought the Lord about this, that it should leave me; but he said to me, 'My grace is sufficient for you, for my power is made perfect in weakness.'" I will all the more gladly boast of my weaknesses, that the power of Christ may rest upon me."

As parents, "arranging" the activities of childhood for our own children, we can see that a "no" is often accompanied by a complementary "yes," and that, as St. Paul boasted, both answers can build our children's character as well as increase their talents. A "no" to ballet class can mean a "yes" to swimming lessons. "No" to taking a walk can mean "yes" to reading books. "No" to more potato chips can mean "yes" to better health. Of course, there are some things for which "no" is the only good answer. Saying "no" to riding a bike without a helmet, for example, can mean "yes" to living another day!

Like I experienced with my parking spot and our unexpected front yard volleyball court, not getting everything we want can be for the best. Rather than stomping our feet and getting mad next time we hear or have to say "no," let's instead start looking around for the accompanying "yes."

Growing Spiritually This Week

1. Describe something that you really wanted and didn't get but now can see was for the best. How long after hearing "no" did it take for you to be able to look back and understand that it was for the best?

2. Read 2 Corinthians 12:7–8. Why didn't God remove St. Paul's thorn in the flesh? What did St. Paul eventually conclude about God's "no"? Was there anything wrong with St. Paul's repeating his request three times?

3. How can saying no to your children be an act of courage and faith? How could you help your children understand that "no" can be a good thing even if they don't want to hear it?

4. Read Luke 22:39–44. What would have been different if God had said "yes" to Jesus' request? In what way did God come to Jesus' aid even though he said "no" to his request? How might we model our prayers after Jesus'?

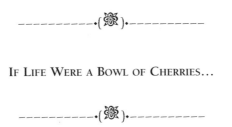

If Life Were a Bowl of Cherries...

In northern Michigan the cherry is the king of all local crops. Every year around the Fourth of July, local cherries are celebrated during the weeklong National Cherry Festival. Ironically, however, there are years when cherries need to be imported for the festival from Washington State because the homegrown cherries are not yet ripe (the festival was moved up from late July several years ago to take advantage of the presence of July 4 tourists).

Commenting on the irony of this situation, a friend observed, "Our contemporary lifestyle doesn't help us understand the seasonality of life. We can have watermelon twelve months of the year because it is imported from Florida or New Zealand when it's not ripe here, but that is not the natural way of fruitfulness of the land—or of fruitfulness in the Lord, which also comes in seasons. We want a steady stream of fruit or blessings from the Lord, like we want a steady steam of watermelon, but just as there are natural seasons for planting, growing, and harvesting, so are there spiritual seasons for waiting, sorrow, blessings, and so forth."

Ecclesiastes 3:1–8 says, "For everything there is a season, and a time for every matter under heaven: a time to be born, and a time to die; a time to plant, and a time to pluck up what is planted; a time to kill, and a time to heal; a time to break down and a time to build up; a time to weep, and a time to laugh; a time to mourn, and a time to dance; a time to cast away stones, and a time to gather stones together; a time to embrace, and a time to refrain from embracing; a time to seek, and a time to lose; a time to keep, and a time to cast away; a time to tear, and a time to sew; a time to keep silence, and a time to speak; a time to love, and a time to hate; a time for war, and a time for peace." The older I grow the better I understand this Scripture, but I still sort of like being able to eat watermelon in January, as I'm sure businesses in northern Michigan really like having the maximum number of visitors attend their cherry festival, even if it means that their local cherries might not be ripe in time.

Not everyone rushes the seasons of life, however. Some personalities are preoccupied with the past. Both rushing and delaying the seasons of our lives, however, can lead to unsatisfactory compromises and sometimes even rob us of the true fruit or blessings of a particular season. Here are some ideas on how to begin living in harmony with our present season of life:

Overcoming a fixation on the future: A fixation on the future may reflect a lack of trust in God's love and his ability to take care of us. One way to overcome this is to maintain a prayer journal consisting of dated prayers and their answers. Reviewing this journal periodically can buoy our confidence that God will be there in the future, just as he was in the past. If we are fixated on the future because we are unhappy with the present, we may need to pray that God would open our eyes to his presence and his provision for us even amid seasons of suffering, scattering, or mourning.

Overcoming a preoccupation with the past: If the past was wonderful, we can let it stand like a well-deserved trophy, but we shouldn't haul it out and polish it at every possible occasion. Instead we should use past triumphs to help ourselves and others bring in new trophies. If the past was regrettable, we urgently need to forgive and move on. Ecclesiastes, quoted above, states that there is a time to give up, to uproot, and to throw away. We can't allow the past to weigh down our dreams like a ball and chain. We only pass through this life once.

This was a great year for northern Michigan. For the first time in many years, the local cherry crop ripened in time for the National Cherry Festival! Seizing the day, we visited a U-Pick orchard where we harvested a satisfying thirty pounds of sweet cherries. Ah, if only all of life was like a bottomless bowl of ripe, sweet cherries…

Growing Spiritually This Week

1. Take some time to reflect on your natural response to time. Which time frame occupies more of your thoughts, the future or the past? Why do you think this is? Make a list of the ways that this impacts how you live in the present, both positively and negatively. How could you make the impact more positive?

2. Read Ecclesiastes 3:1–8. Count how many different "times" or seasons are listed in these verses. Are you in the midst of one of these seasons right now? Which one? Are you able to recognize God's presence in this season? List some ways you could recognize his presence even more.

="3"

3. Make a list of the opposite seasons of life listed in Ecclesiastes. How can understanding the seasonal nature of God's creation help us understand the seasonal nature of human life?

4. Is there a way you can tangibly incorporate seasonal living into your life by doing things like shopping for all your produce at a local farmer's market or by changing your prayer routine to make it coincide with the liturgical season of the Church year? What else might you do to practice living life in its season?

Building Our Children's Character

I love hiking in New England. Enormous sugar maples, towering pines, granite cliffs, sandy beaches, and scenic vistas dot the entire region. I love the rock walls that crisscross nearly every landscape, plunging off even into the deepest woods. When we first moved to the region, I must admit that I was baffled as to why anyone would labor so hard to build a rock wall in the middle of the woods. It didn't take long (and only a few snickers) for a New England native to point out to this Midwestern foreigner that the rock walls had been built after old growth forests had been cleared for farmland by the first generation of European settlers, but before new growth forests had reclaimed the land when subsequent generations of farmers had packed up their wagons and rolled westward to the less rocky Ohio River Valley and beyond.

Looking at the woods with this new knowledge, I could see that many of the mature trees were completely bent around the rock walls, something that could only happen if the walls predated the saplings. Hiking with the family one day, daydreaming about the lifespan of the rock walls, it occurred to me that parenting or building our children's character is in many ways like building a rock wall. There are three steps to both processes:

- Step One is to pick the rocks out of the field. Early settlers labored intensely to pick the rocks out of their fields by hand. These rocks could only be good if they were on the sides of the fields, not in the middle. In parenting terms, these rocks represent the character traits we handpick to teach our children. Examples of character traits are obedience, truthfulness, faithfulness, resourcefulness, generosity, and diligence; every family will consciously or unconsciously emphasize those traits they consider to be most important.

- Step Two is to stack the rocks in a line, making a recognizable boundary. In farming, rock walls were established to mark land boundaries and contain farm animals. In parenting terms, rock walls symbolize the collection of rules we establish in our home in order to teach the handpicked character traits of Step One. Family rules include things like bedtimes, household chores, eating habits, allowance, church attendance, and writing thank-you notes. If we picture our children as livestock (an image to which some may object and others may heartily agree), we can easily see that family rules that are well thought out and consistently applied are like rocks arranged in a wall. They are useful and loving boundaries, which can safely contain growing children.

- Step Three is to maintain the established rock wall. In farming terms, this means regular trips around the perimeter of one's property to repair any breaches in the walls. In parenting terms, this means deciding on the methods of discipline we will use to enforce the family rules we established in Step Two. Methods of discipline include deciding how to communicate family rules, how to motivate our kids to follow them, and what happens if the rules are broken. Specific examples include things like time-outs, spankings, and posting charts of a child's responsibilities. Regularly reinforcing family rules and establishing routine consequences for any breaches helps to keep the entire system of discipline intact and working smoothly.

Like rocks scattered haphazardly throughout farm fields, sometimes-taught character traits or sometimes-enforced rules are not helpful in the cultivation and growth of our children's character. Like building a rock wall, parenting as I've described it here initially involves a lot of backbreaking, mind-bending, and time-consuming labor, but the results are lasting. When I hike through the New England woods, I praise God for the omnipresent rock walls. Steadfast, silent reminders of an era gone by, they encourage me to choose well, to assemble in an orderly fashion, and to apply consistently the character traits I want fixed in my children long after I am gone from their daily lives.

Growing Spiritually This Week

1. Read Deuteronomy 6:4–9. These are God's instructions to the Israelites on child rearing. Record the actions that the Israelites are told to take in raising children from these verses. Do you think these apply to us today? Why or why not?

2. Write the three steps of building your children's character in your journal, leaving a good amount of space between each one. Today, write as many character traits as you can come up with that you would like to teach your children. Circle the most important three.

3. Write as many family rules as you can come up with that you would like to use in teaching your children the character traits you'd like them to have. Circle the most important three.

4. Write as many methods of discipline you can think of that you would like to use in teaching your children the character traits you'd like them to have. Circle the most important three. After completing this week's reflections, it would be helpful to have a conversation with your spouse about what you have learned and written over the week.

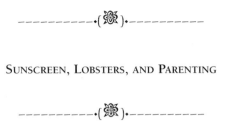

SUNSCREEN, LOBSTERS, AND PARENTING

Heading out for an all-day, multifamily excursion to the beach, I tossed a bottle of sunscreen in the back of the van and told the kids to lather up. Twelve hours later, my nine-year-old was crying in pain as I tried to soothe her lobster-colored skin with aloe. I was really upset with myself. How could I have missed the fact that she hadn't applied sunscreen? We were together all day! The painful incident for my little girl reminded me that, as Christian parents, being physically present to our kids is just the first step. Actively engaging with them is the real goal. Unfortunately—and for a wide variety of reasons—just like this sunscreen episode, it can be pretty easy to be physically present to our kids but emotionally, intellectually, and even spiritually detached.

Examples of this—examples I myself have been guilty of at one time or another—are chitchatting on the phone while playing with the kids, concentrating too much on projects around the house, housecleaning, and/or working at my computer, and the classic example, chewing the fat on the sidelines of a game instead of cheering on my junior athletes. TV shows and shopping can similarly pull our attention away from our kids.

Some of the things I mentioned above have to get done. It's impossible, not to mention unhealthy, to dote on our kids 24/7. However, if we review the time we've spent with our children and see that it contains more time than not spent putting them off, telling them to go play quietly, or plugging them into another TV show or video game, then we are kind of missing the point of being with them.

To help myself stay on task in this area of parenting, I have come up with different plans over the years. The plan that has worked the best is to schedule five short periods a day when I am completely available and intensely present to my kids. Obviously, these are not the only times I am engaged with the kids, but by being sure that I am engaged during these times, I am usually able to stay in touch with their needs and give them focused attention even on the busiest of days. I scheduled these periods to coincide with times when we are either reconvening after being apart, going in separate directions after being together, or eating together. Basically, what I am doing is called "starting off on the right foot" or "parting on a good note." Christian psychologist and author Dr. James Dobson, writes in *Focus on the Family* magazine, "When we have been apart from those we love, we have an opportunity to reset the mood. It all depends on the first five minutes [of getting back together]" (and the last five minutes of sending each other off, I would add). Here are the time periods I came up with:

- **Greet the Day** is when we first see each other in the morning. We routinely hug and say, "Good morning; how did you sleep?"
- **Meet the Day** is when we say or sing prayers at breakfast, and I bless those departing the home.

- **Embrace the Day** happens around midafternoon over a snack (after naps or school). We pause to sit together and ready ourselves for an afternoon of cocurricular activities.
- **Discuss the Day** happens over family dinnertime.
- **Close the Day** is when we read books together, say or sing prayers, and bless one another before bedtime.

No matter what else I have to get done in a day, it is my goal to be engaged with each child physically, emotionally, intellectually, and spiritually at these five junctures every day. Sometimes things slip and I get distracted, like the day my nine-year-old got cooked like a lobster. Over the years, however, having this plan has helped me get back on track fairly quickly, without experiencing too many whole family lobster bakes.

Growing Spiritually This Week

1. Recall a time when you found out too late that you had missed an important detail in parenting (feeding, helping with schoolwork, keeping someone safe). How did it happen? How have you not (or how might you not) repeat that experience?

2. In the *Catechism of the Catholic Church*, #2228, we read, "Parents' respect and affection are expressed by the care and attention they devote to bringing up their young children and providing for their physical and spiritual needs." How do you care for the physical needs of each of your children? How do you provide for their collective physical needs?

3. How do you provide for the spiritual needs of your individual children? How do you provide for their collective spiritual needs?

4. In what ways are providing for the physical and spiritual needs of our children connected? What additional aspects of parenting come into play when we consider their emotional or psychological needs?

THE NATURE OF CHRISTIAN UNITY: PART ONE

There I stood, in the cool shadows of the towering pine trees overlooking a small beaver pond in the twilight of the day. Gathered with me at this "vesper" service at the Au Sable Institute of Environmental Studies, singing hymns of praise and worship to our Lord, were sixty Christians from several different countries and many different denominations. Multiple vocal and instrumental harmonies joyously rose up to meet the swaying pine branches. On one side of me, an elderly lady raised her thin, angel-like voice in praise, while on the other side, my husband offered up his praise in deep, rich tones. Chattering squirrels, croaking frogs, and the forlorn call of a loon joined in our harmonies. I closed my eyes and was swept into the beauty of the moment; the beauty of praising God in harmony with other Christians surrounded by the splendor of God's creation.

In my mind's eye, I saw images of unity; first, there were colorful waves of grain stretching from horizon to horizon. Red, brown, yellow, black, and white under the sun and in the shadows, the grains were bending and bowing, swaying and dancing in harmony as the wind rushed over them. Rushing through the fields, I saw a shallow stream separate into countless cool-blue meanders. The meanders continuously joined back up, separated, and rejoined as they traveled closer and closer to the sea. By the end of their journey, the multihued ribbons of fresh blue water were braided, flowing together to meet and mingle with the salty waves of the ocean. The harmonies I heard and the images of natural unity I saw produced a great longing in my heart for true communion with the friends I stood among.

Unity among Christians, or ecumenism, is one of the most important issues of our age. Christian unity is of utmost importance to a harmonious family life, especially when interdenominational marriages bring believers of other creeds into our extended family circles. Disunity among Christians is something most of us have probably experienced—if not with family, then with neighbors, friends, or coworkers. I can remember stories from the early 1900s about children being disowned—or at least bringing shame on their parents and themselves—for marrying outside their parents' denomination.

Since the closing of the Second Vatican Council in 1965, and due most recently to the prayer and labor of the late Pope John Paul II, fewer of the extremes of that discord and disowning have followed us into the twenty-first century. Since 1965, the Catholic Church has been officially working hard to heal the wounds that two great schisms and many small splinterings have inflicted on the body of Christ, and she has been asking her members to do the same. The Church has embraced ecumenism, because in the words of the Second Vatican Council's *Unitatis Redintegratio* ("Decree on Ecumenism"), "Nevertheless, our separated brethren, whether considered as individuals or as Communities and Churches, are not blessed with that unity which Jesus Christ wished to bestow on all those who through Him were born again into one body."

In other words, the Catholic Church desires Christian unity because Jesus wished to bestow such unity on us. In fact, unity was one of his final prayers for his followers. Right after the Last Supper, Jesus said: "I do not pray for these [twelve apostles] only, but also for those who believe in me through their word, that they may all be one; even as thou, Father, art in me, and I in thee, that they also may be in us, so that the world may believe that thou hast sent me" (John 17:20–21).

Like the images I envisioned at vespers in the woods, Jesus used images from nature (a grapevine and its branches, for example) to demonstrate the goodness and ability of many separate parts bearing fruit individually—but only when they are all tied back into him. Other images echo the same goodness: many instruments forming one orchestra, many colors of thread being woven into one piece of cloth, or many cords forming one strong rope. Having shared a vision for the potential of Christian unity with these images, I'll move in the next devotional from the lofty vision of Christian unity to some concrete ways that we can promote that unity in our own families.

Growing Spiritually This Week

1. There are so many images of unity in nature. Which are your favorite and why?

2. In what ways is teaching your children about ecumenism an important aspect of teaching them the Catholic faith? From what Catholic sources could you get accurate information on the teachings of other

Christian denominations before talking to your children about them?

3. How would being better acquainted with the teachings of the Catholic Church better equip you for true friendship and honest dialog with other Christians? How would it help you educate your children in becoming strong Catholics and embracing ecumenism?

4. Imagine that you are God. How would you feel about the discord and lack of harmony among your earthly children? As a parent, what would you do to reunite your children? Is God asking you to do these things with believers of different Christian denominations?

The Nature of Christian Unity: Part Two

In the last reflection, I wrote about a beautiful, ecumenical praise and worship service I attended under a canopy of pine trees. The setting was the Big Woods of northern Michigan where my husband teaches a college course in land resources at Au Sable Institute of Environmental Studies during the first part of each summer. Au Sable Institute is a small, scientific field station that serves a consortium of about fifty Christian colleges. For six of the past eight years, our family has been blessed to make the trek to this northern woods academic retreat, which is why the kids and I happened to be at the outdoor service known as "vespers" that I described last week.

The Institute is staffed primarily by believers from evangelical denominations, and the majority of the students enrolled are from mainline Protestant or evangelical colleges in the U.S. and Canada, often including several African students and children of missionaries. We are the only entirely Catholic family in the community, a situation that has opened us up to many fulfilling friendships and some occasional anti-Catholic prejudice. No matter which extreme we've experienced, living so closely among such a wide range of Christians has been a tremendous blessing. It has given us a lived understanding of—and a real heart for—the furthering of understanding, cooperation, and unity among members of different Christian denominations (a pursuit also known as ecumenism).

Presented in Rome at St. Peter's Basilica on November 21, 1964, the opening statement of the Catholic Church's *Unitatis Redintegratio* ("Decree on Ecumenism") reads as follows:

> The restoration of unity among all Christians is one of the principal concerns of the Second Vatican Council. Christ the Lord founded one Church and one Church only. However, many Christian communions present themselves to men as the true inheritors of Jesus Christ; all indeed profess to be followers of the Lord but differ in mind and go their different ways, as if Christ Himself were divided. Such division openly contradicts the will of Christ, scandalizes the world, and damages the holy cause of preaching the Gospel to every creature.

Even if you've never been the only Catholic in the group, you've probably experienced the difficulty, discord, and even scandal of interdenominational relationships. It's not easy. Based on my interdenominational experiences, here are some ways we can engage our heads, hearts, and hands in promoting ecumenism and improving interdenominational relationships within our own families and beyond.

We can engage our heads by reading *Unitatis Redintegratio* (Decree on Ecumenism) for ourselves. It is beautifully clear and only takes about fifteen minutes to read. You can find it easily by doing a Google search on "Second Vatican Council Decree on Ecumenism" on the Internet.

By reading this document and other similar ones, we can develop a profound love of the Roman Catholic Church and a working knowledge of her doctrinal traditions and diverse cultural history. We can build up true unity and avoid false unity by learning the essential, creed-based differences and the nonessential, behavioral differences between denominations.

We can engage our hearts by showing honest respect for non-Catholic Christians. We can become students of the Bible; it is the backbone of all Christian churches. We can humbly admit to the strengths and weaknesses within our own Church and other denominations, too. We can apologize for negative experiences others might have had with Catholicism, and we can become a positive connection to our Church for them.

We can engage our hands by serving with Christians of all stripes at soup kitchens and food pantries, by helping with pro-life ministries, and by celebrating communal Thanksgiving services or prayer breakfasts. We can share resources, such as good Christian music and Christian fiction.

As we set about the task of ecumenism, we must remember that Christian disunity "damages the holy cause of preaching the Gospel to every creature." By remembering images of unity in nature like the grapevine whose many branches have unity through their connection to the vine itself, we can continue to pray for unity even if actual ecumenical relationships are complex and problematic. If Jesus is the Vine and we are the branches, as Jesus says in John 15:5, then the most important thing we have in common with other Christians is Jesus, the agreed-upon life-giver of us all.

Growing Spiritually This Week

1. Make a list of all the different Christian denominations attended by individuals in your extended family. How many are there? Also list the denominations of your Christian coworkers and friends. Which of these are the most like Catholicism and which are most different?

2. Describe some of the best friendships or interactions you've had with non-Catholic Christians. Describe some of the worst. What do you think made the difference between the best and the worst?

3. Read John 17:20–23. What is Jesus' most heartfelt prayer for those who would come to believe in him through the apostles' teaching? Why do you think this is? How could you defuse potential arguments about the different teachings of Christian churches?

4. Even within the same church, petty divisions can arise. Name some of the nonessential differences that exist in your church, and list some ways you could bring healing, not division, to the individuals involved.

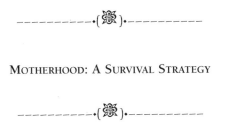

MOTHERHOOD: A SURVIVAL STRATEGY

OK, moms, time for a pop quiz. Using common sense, answer the following question: Given the choice between swimming, treading water, or remaining still, which would you choose as the best survival strategy if you found yourself wearing a life preserver and floating in the middle of a frigid body of water (lake, ocean, etc.)? Do not peek at the answer before answering for yourself. Remember, your goal is to stay alive.

Time's up! Here's the answer: In cold water, loss of body heat will be your biggest enemy, so the correct but surprisingly contradictory answer is to float as still as possible! According to the U.S. Coast Guard, the best way to keep the core of your body warm in a situation like this is to hug your knees to your chest, thereby creating a little pool of water in front of yourself that is warmed by and, in turn, warms your middle. Thrashing your arms and legs around by trying to swim or even treading water will only cause you to lose body heat more quickly.

Before participating in a Coast Guard survival lesson on Lake Michigan, I would have bet a million dollars that the only chance of survival in such a situation would have been to keep moving—

by either swimming or treading water—but definitely not just holding still. Had I found myself thrown overboard without expert preparation and followed my instincts, my choice would have been—literally— dead wrong.

What has this got to do with motherhood, the real topic of this reflection? Learning to rethink one's survival strategy and embrace what may seem to defy common sense can be of critical, life-sustaining importance when it comes to surviving motherhood—a situation that I'll bet most women are thrown into with little or no expert preparation.

The parallel between surviving motherhood and surviving in cold water is an especially strong one for me. Since my first child was born nearly nineteen years ago, the one emotion I have found myself repeatedly battling is the feeling of being in over my head and nearly swallowed up by the demands of the job.

With my first child's birth, there was the overwhelming awareness that this precious newborn was being kept alive by my milk alone. Help! It was just so much responsibility for an inexperienced, newly born mother. What was the nurse thinking when she put that bundle in my arms and wheeled my daughter and me out of the hospital?

Nineteen months later, her brother arrived. By then, I knew I could keep him alive, but my daughter was now a toddler who climbed, jumped, and hurled herself off tall objects while I was feeding him. Oh, double help! As the years have added up, so have the responsibilities. I now have six children and at least six laundry baskets of clothes that need cleaning twice a week. I need at least two grocery carts or a flatbed at BJ's to haul home just a week's worth of groceries. Homeschooling curriculum guides, sports schedules, and orthodontic bills flood in.

Plus, doesn't everyone know that there's a lot of worrying to be done? Does each of the kids have a personal relationship with Jesus yet? Are they each being challenged academically? Do they have good friendships? Are we eating foods that are healthy enough?

"Be still and know that I am God." I have read that quote from Psalm 46 on a million cutesy coffee mugs and t-shirts, but I have never understood it. It's not logical. It's not common sense. I've got too much to do. It must not apply to mothers. I've got to keep moving or I'll drown under all the responsibilities....

Rest. Be still. Stop thrashing. Give yourself a hug. Sit down together for a family meal. Stop by church for daily Mass. Read the funny papers. None of it is common sense, but it is the Coast Guard –approved cold-water survival strategy that I would have never guessed to be correct, and it's the life survival technique that the Bible has been recommending for thousands of years. Hmmm... maybe it's time to set aside some of our own "common sense" and take some expert advice.

Growing Spiritually This Week

1. What experiences have you had in survival tactics—perhaps with boats, camping in the wilderness, or working in the inner city? How would you compare these experiences with your experiences of motherhood?

2. Read Psalm 46. Meditate on the image of God as your refuge, then on God as your strength, and finally on God as your ever-present help in trouble. What views of God do these individual images give you?

3. List three specific parenting issues that are stressing you out today. How might the truth that God is your refuge, your strength, and your ever-present help in trouble be applied to these three specific stresses?

4. Spend your prayer time today artistically inscribing Psalm 46:10 ("Be still and know that I am God") in your journal.

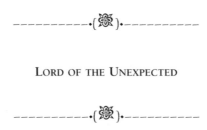

Lord of the Unexpected

Over the summer, I took portraits of a young couple and their adorable, eighteen-month-old son. On our drive to a nearby public garden, the little guy fell asleep in the car, so I decided to first take pictures of Mom and Dad while the boy's aunt remained with him in the car. Strolling through the tranquil garden, we settled upon the perfect backdrop: a picturesque dock extending into a glass-calm lake. Geese gracefully floated by. Sunlight sparkled off the deep blue water. All in all, it took about five minutes to capture some stunning portraits of the couple.

Jokingly I said to them, "You two look so peaceful; just sit still. I'll go get your son, slip him onto your laps, and we'll be done in no time." Of course, we all knew better and shared a healthy chuckle at the idea of being able to simply "slip" a child into the scene without unsettling the existing composition. The point was adequately proven as it took four adults another hour and a half to obtain first-rate portraits of Mr. Adorable.

Like the presence of children, it seems to me that the Lord God's presence in our lives is often unsettling. We want the Lord to come into our lives, to sit nicely and quietly, not disturbing our preexisting plans, ideals, and methods. In short, we want the Lord to behave. But God does not sit quietly. Like an eighteen-month-old child, he is always on the move. Like handfuls of rocks thrown into glassy calm water, the Lord often uses disturbing events to catch our attention and stop us from being so self-contented. Even a quick read through the Beatitudes or the lives of the Old Testament prophets like Moses, St. Paul, and many of the saints reveals that the Lord almost seems to delight in paradoxical events that turn our worlds upside down.

I am especially in tune with the unanticipated things of life, because we recently were surprised to find ourselves expecting Bratton Baby #6! Unlike the couple waiting on the dock, the gift of a sixth child was not at all what my husband or I were expecting at this time in our lives, and, speaking frankly, I've been angry with the Lord, struggling to understand this sudden curveball.

As the initial shock has passed, however, I've been thinking that it's really not Bratton Baby #6 who is unexpected, it's God who is, yet again, working in an unexpected way. Commenting on the Lord's unexpected methods, author John Shea writes, "Martha (the biblical sister of Mary) welcomed Jesus into her home. Her home is not merely her house, her physical dwelling. It is her whole way of thinking and acting. In order to make Martha's home the Lord's dwelling, the Lord will have to correct the way Martha thinks and acts. But this correction is not unwanted criticism. She asked the Lord in; and although what follows will not be what she expects, it will be what she invited."

My husband and I invited the Lord into our married lives on our wedding day. Having heard a knock, we opened the door, welcomed Jesus in, and gave him permission to be the Lord of our joint life.

Nonetheless, like Martha, we were not at all prepared for such a bold houseguest as Jesus has turned out to be. Twenty weeks of pregnancy have shown me, once again, just how much I love my own will, worship my own plans, and adore being in control of my own destiny—but also just how badly the Lord God wants me to refocus, love, worship, and adore only him.

For me, having Baby #6 is a dramatic, life-changing, refocusing event. Being in tune with the unexpected, however, I've become more aware of the Lord's refocusing others' lives through unexpected, often more heartrending events. I spoke with a father of four whose wife died of cancer only eight months after being diagnosed, cried with a mother of three whose husband took a mistress, sent an encouraging note to a father of eight who couldn't find a job, and emailed a missionary who was forced to leave the mission field due to illness. It wasn't until this past Sunday at Mass, however, when I reached out during the Our Father to hold the hand of a young girl next to me only to feel a smooth stump at the end of her wrist, that I suffered true shame at my questioning anger with the Lord over the unexpected nature of this pregnancy. For the first time, my self-righteous heart was broken and I whispered, "Oh, dear Lord, who am I to question? Please give me a new heart. Make it as graceful and as accepting of my life as the one you've given this beautiful young girl."

In one sense, Bratton Baby #6 changes everything about the predictable portrait of life I had imagined and was expecting for my husband and me and our five, preexisting children. In another sense, it's not the baby at all but the One I call Lord who has unexpectedly changed everything, and it is I who invited him to do it.

Growing Spiritually This Week

1. How do you feel about throwing parties at your house? Which do you find more stressful, planning and preparing for the party or entertaining the guests once the party has begun? Why?

2. Read Luke 10:39–41. Like Martha, we may desire to have Jesus in our homes and hearts but still not want to change our plans to accommodate the way he thinks and acts. Think of an unexpected event in your life. What did you learn about God in the midst of it? About yourself?

3. In what ways is Jesus a resident member of your marriage? In what ways is he an unexpected guest? How could you invite Jesus in to your marriage more often and more deeply?

4. In what unexpected ways is God on the move in your life right now? Are you filled with joy or anxiety about this movement? If you are feeling anxious, what might you do to overcome your anxiety and reach a place of joyful anticipation instead?

Katrina, Divorce, and Other Unnatural Disasters

When is the right time to take action? And when the right time comes, what are the right actions to take? These are the types of questions with which Americans rightfully wrestle after natural disasters such as Hurricane Katrina, which ravaged New Orleans and the Gulf Coast several years ago (and more recently the tragedy of the Gulf oil spill). What could have been done to prevent the ensuing devastation? Who was in charge, and why didn't this authority do the right thing at the right time? Nursing homes were sued for the deaths of elderly patients. The head of FEMA, the federal agency theoretically in charge, resigned under pressure. Government agencies still shuffled blame around like a hot potato.

Following the news of Hurricane Katrina was particularly tough for me because at the time I was asking the same types of responsibility questions about a similar kind of disaster. The disaster I'm referring to is divorce, which has ripped through and turned upside down the lives of several families I hold dear. The saddest part for me is that there was so much that could have been done to prevent some of the human devastation of both Katrina and the divorces I've witnessed.

The New Orleans catastrophe was far from unforeseen, according to *Time* magazine, and many other news outlets. The city of New Orleans knew about the inadequacies of its levee system. New Orleans knew about its nursing homes that had been built below sea level. Most of all, it's no secret that New Orleans sits at the top of the Caribbean's hurricane alley. Not one but many heads turned the other way when it came to forestalling the disaster that engulfed New Orleans during and after Hurricane Katrina.

Most disasters, whether natural or manmade, do not pop up out of the blue. With the divorce rate at an appalling 50 percent in this country, no couple can take for granted that their marriage exists safely outside the realm of divorce. In the marriages I've seen succumb to the torrents of divorce, there were many, many warning signs. The marriage was either built on a flawed foundation, or had cracked over time in several vital areas.

So, when is the right time to take action on the threat of divorce? Now. Right now! No matter how in love with our spouses we feel today, marriage and family life sit on the top of Satan's list of things to destroy. As sure as hurricanes form in the Caribbean, marital conflict will sweep over and test the strength of our marriages from time to time. It's not a question of if—but when.

No spouse wants to say, "Hey, Sweetie, let's pull the family out of most of our non-work commitments so we can be sure to have a date every week." Yet if we don't, months can slip by before we ever have a meaningful conversation. No spouse is eager to admit, "Hey, Honey, your travel schedule leaves me lonely and vulnerable to the attention of this new person I met at the gym." Yet, this is exactly the type of thing that needs to be discussed openly, or it will begin the undoing of our marriages.

We must learn from the undoing of New Orleans in the face of Hurricane Katrina. The right time to take preventive measures against the storm of divorce is not when the storm is looming on the horizon. The right time is when the skies are still blue and our marriages are still bright. Fortunately, there are gazillions of measures we can take to shore up and save our marriages from ruin. We can affirm the good that is already in our spouses. We can take responsibility for the discord we've caused, ask for forgiveness, and expect the same in return. We can build unity by praying together. We can make time to have fun together. We can stop hiding behind the facade of busyness and address the weaker or even dysfunctional parts of our relationship head-on. Although severe storms are natural parts of the physical world and upsetting squalls are known to besiege the best of marriages, devastation and divorce do not have to be the inevitable aftermath.

Growing Spiritually This Week

1. If you are married, make a list of the qualities that you love most in your spouse. Be generous, and forget about that misunderstanding from last week. If you are not married, make a dream list of qualities you'd like to have in a spouse.

2. Rank your list of spousal qualities (actual or dream). Briefly write why each quality ranks where it does on your list. If you are married, affirm your spouse by sharing your list and ranking it with him or her this week.

3. No marriage is perfect. What three big issues and what three little issues are looming in your marriage? What preventative measures could you take to stop these issues from continuing to damage to your marriage? If you are not married, think of a good marriage which you have experienced firsthand. Try to list as many reasons as you can for the lasting goodness in this relationship.

4. What is your experience of marital counseling? If you are married, what might be gained if you and your spouse were to meet with a marriage counselor or go on an organized marriage retreat? If you are not married, how might you encourage one specific married couple?

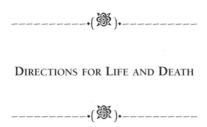

Directions for Life and Death

I was in the middle of a life-or-death crisis, and I had no idea where to turn. Literally, I didn't know where to turn as I idled at a red light, completely disorientated, somewhere in the middle of the godforsaken concrete jungle known as Boston. Tears pooled on two pieces of paper in my lap; a map to Children's Hospital and directions to Massachusetts General Hospital (MGH).

Earlier that morning, my seven-year-old son had been whisked up to Boston from our hospital on Cape Cod by ambulance. I thought he had been sent to Children's, and I had said so to some good friends, who immediately drove over to our house with a computer map showing me how to get there. As I approached the city, however, I realized that the written directions from Falmouth Hospital indicated that my son had been sent to MGH, not Children's. So there I sat with a tear-smeared map to the wrong place, tear-smudged directions to the right place, and not a clue as to where I was in relation to either one.

My emotional condition was not helped by the fact that I had been awake for nearly forty-eight hours, nor that our emergency room marathon had come on the heels of a distressing church event and an exhausting two-week visit from extended family. Despair, fatigue, and fear wrapped around my thoughts like sweaty fingers, as I tried in vain to figure out what to do when the light turned green. All I wanted was to be with my son. The short version of what had happened was that my son's appendix had burst about ten days earlier and a severe abdominal infection had begun to brew in his little body. Two surgeries, fifteen days in the hospital, and a year later, my son is absolutely fine, thanks be to God.

After my first panic-ridden drive through Boston, I became proficient at getting in and out of the city. I learned when to stay in the right-hand lane and when to move to the left-hand lane. I learned to leave the Cape at 6:00 AM if I wanted to beat rush hour and arrive in time to talk to the doctors during their morning rounds. I learned not to drink a thirty-six ounce cup of coffee on the drive up and hope to make it to the hospital without having an emergency of my own. If I had only known all this before I was under such emotional stress! Of course, I had no reason to think in advance that my son's appendix would burst, and therefore no reason to prepare for it ahead of time. We, however, all have this terminal condition called "life-on-earth." We all have every reason to anticipate involvement in the deaths of some of our loved ones, not to mention our own death.

I know, that's not a comforting turn to my story, but the experience with my son led me to believe that it is important that we learn some of the basic Catholic moral directions concerning end-of-life issues before we are in the emotional situation of having to use them. We are so blessed as Catholics to belong to a Church that does not leave us on our own, but leads us by the hand with sound medical directions that are based in both holy Scripture and modern science.

Here's the thing: trusting ourselves to make good decisions under emotional stress is like trusting that there will be no Monday morning traffic jam in Boston. It could happen, but the odds are not in our favor. If we will take time now to learn some basic Catholic directions for end-of-life issues, we will be less likely to ask for, accept, or follow faulty directions from well-intended but misinformed sources (like I did with geographical directions). Plus, we will be more proficient in applying the directions when needed, giving us what we really want, which is as much time as possible with our loved ones. Excellent information about many end-of-life issues can easily be found at the "In Support of Life" section of the Massachusetts Catholic Conference's website (www.macathconf.org).

Growing Spiritually This Week

1. How often do you think about death and heaven? What feelings do you have regarding death? Scripture talks about death often. What can we know about it from the following Bible passages: John 5:26, Romans 6:9–11, Romans 6:23, Revelations 21:4?

2. What steps have you taken to be prepared for your own death? If you have experienced the death of a loved one, did you feel panicked or prepared? If you felt prepared, what helped you feel that way?

3. Write out three or more questions you have about handling the medical process of death and dying.

4. Log on to www.embracingourdying.com. Browse the site for fifteen minutes in order to find answers to the questions you wrote for Question Three.

---------•(❀)•---------

Harvesting Faith at Home:
Reflections for Ordinary Time in Autumn

---------•(❀)•---------

CHILDHOOD AS A MOSAIC

Mosaic art is incredible. While visiting the Basilica of the National Shrine of the Immaculate Conception in Washington, D.C., the family and I stood gaping at the intricate mosaic of Christ in Majesty behind the main altar. From a distance, nearly three million tiny pieces merged to create a powerful image of Christ that left us breathless.

We were in awe, in part, because we had dabbled in mosaic art while studying the Middle Ages in our homeschool curriculum, and let me tell you, it is not easy! It was hard enough for us to make simple geometric designs; we couldn't imagine being able to make the 3,600-square-foot IMAX mosaic in front of us.

Looking at a mosaic up close, the artist's choice of shape and color are not intrinsically logical. The artistry of creating a mosaic lies in the artist's ability to be mindful of the big picture while working on only a small portion; in giving adequate attention to the details of one tile at a time before moving too quickly to the next.

I think childhood is a large mosaic with parents as the primary artists. The individual tiles are the experiences we provide for our children. The colors of the tiles are the heart attitudes we have while properly placing those experiences. The challenge of parenting, then, is threefold: 1) having a vision for the type of childhood we want for our children; 2) choosing and cementing in place the experiences that will add up to the big picture of childhood that we've chosen; and 3) coloring the entire picture with the Christian virtues of faith, hope, and love.

Parents will not, of course, have complete control over every experience and attitude their child encounters. But rather than this reality letting parents off the hook, it only highlights how important it is that parents purposefully choose good shapes and pleasing colors when they do have the choice.

Are we committed to our marriages? The most important piece of any happy childhood is a mom and a dad who love one another and who work at keeping that love alive. Are we committed to the work of family life? Continually surrounding our kids with love, structure, and discipline takes diligence and is not always fun, but it is a big part of creating a safe and happy home. Simple things like eating dinner together or taking walks or bike rides together, laid side by side over an entire childhood, will create beautiful memories of love and family togetherness from which our children will draw strength for the rest of their lives.

Where will we live? How many children will we have? How will we educate our children? Will one parent work or two? Do we have extended family that can positively contribute to our family life? These are the details that will form the mosaic of our child's childhood. These are the details to which we must give some thought. For some of these lifestyle choices, there is no one-size-fits-all answer. We do not have to do what our parents did nor what our friends are doing. We do have to think and pray about the overall mosaic that we want to create, or we may end up with an unintentional hodgepodge instead of a purposeful design.

With the idea of a mosaic in mind, it is easy for me to understand why Jesus emphasized that obeying the spirit of the law is as essential as obeying the letter of the law. The same shapes will create an entirely different mosaic if they are colored with shades of blue and green, say, instead of orange and red; doubt, despair, and disinterest instead of faith, hope, and love. Color represents our heart attitude. Doing a little self-evaluation can help us assess the attitudes that are coloring the tiles of our children's mosaics. We need to seek God's help and guidance in designing and fabricating a happy and holy childhood for our little (and not so little) ones, one mosaic piece at a time. When we finally do get to see the big picture, our attention to the daily details will have made a big difference. I hope your mosaic takes your breath away!

Growing Spiritually This Week

1. Do you consider yourself an artistic person? What things do you like to create? In what ways do you try to "color" your home and family life with faith? With hope? With love? With humor? With generosity? With what other virtues and values do you color your children's world?

2. Draw a picture or a series of symbols, or design a flag or family shield that represents the "big picture" of the childhood you want to create for your children.

3. Consider the lifestyle choices mentioned in this week's reflection—where you live, how you educate your children, your work schedules, etc. In which of these areas is your family positively different from the family in which you grew up?

4. On a scale of one to ten, how content are you with your current lifestyle choices? How would you rate their being in line with God's will for your family? What steps could you take to improve that rating, if necessary?

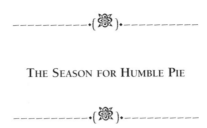

The Season for Humble Pie

It's that time of year again, the season for pie. The delicious time of year when I begin to crave warm apple pie with vanilla ice cream melting on top, piping hot turkey potpie with lots of gravy, and pumpkin pie with whipped cream and a cup of steaming apple cider. Of course, in the middle of June you'll hear me give the same rallying cry for pie, but at that time of year it's for fresh strawberry-rhubarb pie. Oh, man, my mouth is watering just thinking about it. In late July, there is nothing better than a fresh blueberry pie with real whipped cream. Well, that is, until August comes along, and peaches are in season. Peach pie is oh-so-very yummy with a glass of cold milk.

Obviously, I love pie. Give me pie and coffee for breakfast, and I'm the happiest woman in the world. Pie with afternoon tea outclasses any other midday snack. Pie for dessert beats all. There is only one kind of pie I don't like: humble pie. No matter how it's prepared, humble pie ends up being just a little too tart for my delicate palate. To tell the truth, when humble pie is being served, I get really "calorie" conscious, and quickly look around for someone with whom to go halves.

Unfortunately, humble pie seems to be God's favorite, and it is "in season" all year long.

The Old Testament tells us "to do justice, and to love kindness, and to walk humbly with your God" (Micah 6:8). The New Testament implores us to "do nothing from selfishness or conceit, but in humility count others better than yourselves" (Philippians 2:3) and "humble yourselves before the Lord and he will exalt you" (James 4:10). According to St. Augustine of Hippo, "Humility is the foundation of all the other virtues." In the "Canticle of the Creatures," St. Francis of Assisi sings, "Praise and bless my Lord, give thanks and serve him in all humility." Obviously, Christians who are serious about growing in their relationships with Jesus need to acquire the taste for humble pie.

My life's experiences lead me to believe that we grow in all virtues—humility included—through experiential education. That is, we learn to be humble after we have pridefully fallen on our faces, stuck our feet in our mouths, or tripped over our own tongues. After we have done this one time too many, we learn that being humble enough to admit our transgressions is far sweeter than being humiliated by their negative consequences. I suspect most married couples come to humility after an overblown argument or two that could have been settled easily and quickly if one of them had simply said, "I'm sorry. I was wrong. Will you forgive me?" Even if our "enemy" is wrong, it does not mean that we are automatically right.

Admitting that we are sinful is not the only way we can practice humility. We know we are on the road to humility when we can let other people take the limelight, head up the project, or get a pat on the back without having to either butt in and toot our own horns, or sulk until someone asks, "What's the matter?" I heard it said once that humility is "knowing our place before God." St. Augustine shows us this place with his expression, "Man is a beggar before God." What a beautiful image! Our proper posture before God is on our knees in humble adoration, not strutting around like peacocks.

It is tempting to say, "Oh, thank you very much, but I'm trying to cut down," when God comes around with humble pie. I think, however, that this is one kind of pie for which we need to forget the virtue diet, forget going halves, and instead say, "Go ahead, Lord, give me a double portion!"

Growing Spiritually This Week

1. What is your favorite kind of pie? Do you have any good memories involving pie? Any other special foods?

2. Consider St. Augustine's quote: "Humility is the foundation of all other virtues." Look at *CCC*, #1833–1845 and make a list of the other virtues St Augustine is referring to.

3. Draw a picture of a pie, labeling the bottom crust as "humility." Assign and label each of the other ingredients of your pie with one of the other seven virtues—the main filling, the sugar, the top crust, the crisp topping, the whipped topping, etc. How is humility the foundation of all this goodness?

4. Read the Scripture passages listed in this reflection from your Bible, and then list some ways that you can grow in Scriptural humility.

Equipping Our Kids for the Soccer Field of Life

"Therefore take the whole armor of God, that you may be able to withstand in the evil day, and having done all, to stand.."
—Ephesians 6:13

All of our kids have played soccer. They love the game! I, on the other hand, am only beginning to understand it. At the start of our first soccer season, years ago, I had no clue what type of equipment the kids really needed to play. Fortunately, the town recreation department issued shin guards and tube socks, but when the kids suggested their need for soccer cleats (like their teammates), I was pretty sure the "need" was really a faddish extra—like sweatbands, only more expensive. Each kid already had a perfectly good pair of tennis shoes, and these seemed good enough to me for running after a large ball on a flat field.

Boy, was I wrong! During the opening few minutes of her first "real" soccer game, our especially enthusiastic six-year-old daughter and her teammates looked like a herd of wildebeests stampeding after this little checkered ball that had a mind of its own. Unfortunately, every time my poor daughter made a quick turn or tried to stop, her feet slid out from under her and the cleated herd trampled her. It was clear that her flat-bottomed tennis shoes weren't going to cut it. She needed to have a little more grabbing and holding power against the other players, or she wasn't going to survive the season in one piece. So, the first thing Mom learned about soccer was that cleats are not faddish extras.

In the New Testament we are instructed, "Therefore, take the whole armor of God, that you may be able to withstand in the evil day, and having done all, to stand" (Ephesians 6:13). Properly equipping kids to stand firm in their Catholic faith is not unlike properly equipping them for a soccer game. Against a stampede of worldly ideas and people, kids need some spiritual cleats for a little Christian grabbing and holding power so every passing herd doesn't trample their faith.

What types of "spiritual cleats" will ground children deeply in their faith in Jesus Christ? Among the most important are formational types of experiences that will leave positive impressions in their minds about the abundant joy and blessings of the Christian life. Here are a few ideas to consider:

- Make going to Mass as natural and desirable as breathing. Don't make attendance a question mark or a battleground every Sunday. Just go, and go joyfully. Go expecting some gift of grace or under-standing from the Lord, because he wants to give it to us.
- Fill your home with good Christian media and music. Listen to contemporary Christian rock music when the kids are teens.

Attend Christian rock concerts together. Watch Christian movies. Read Christian periodicals and newspapers.

- Pray. Pray with your kids. Pray for others. Pray for healing, for forgiveness, and in thanksgiving. Try different styles of prayer; perhaps the Rosary, perhaps extemporaneous prayer. Charismatic and contemplative prayer are both parts of our Catholic heritage. Try them.

- Cultivate in your family a love of Holy Scripture. Read Bible stories to the kids from birth, and give them their own, age-appropriate Bibles. Attend Bible study groups.

- Love your spouse. Love your neighbors. Hold your tongue. Show with your actions, as well as your words, that Jesus is the Lord of your life.

- Give your kids role models of Catholicism. Teach them about the saints of long ago and the missionaries of today. Put up posters of Catholic heroes in their bedrooms, right next to the sports heroes and movie stars! You might even take down one or two of the secular posters to make room.

- Do good deeds in the name of Jesus. Get your whole family involved in a neighborhood missions project. Financially support missionaries.

By visualizing each of these ideas as a single prong on the bottom of a pair of spiritual cleats, we can see that the more prongs the cleats have and the stronger each prong is, the less our kids will slip and slide on the soccer field of life. Spiritual cleats are not faddish extras for Catholic kids; they are necessary equipment for the game.

Growing Spiritually This Week

1. If you have soccer cleats in the house (football shoes or other cleated shoes will work too), grab one and look at it. How many cleats are there? How long are the cleats? How thick? How do you think the cleats enable players to perform better in their sport?

2. Look up Ephesians 6:10–18 and write it in your journal. What is the stated purpose of taking up the full armor of God? What difficulties have you experienced in standing up for your faith-based decisions? How might taking up the whole armor of God help you stand firm?

3. Draw a picture of yourself as the Christian warrior described in Ephesians 6:10–18. Be sure to outfit yourself with all six components of the full armor of God.

4. Reread the devotion from this week, paying special attention to the ideas that represent each spiritual cleat. Congratulate yourself on any ideas that you have already put in place in your home. Write in your journal any ideas you like but have not yet incorporated into your home. How do you think these would help you and your children stand firm in the Catholic faith?

QUENCHING OUR CHILDREN'S THIRST

We were about twenty minutes into a daylong Catholic tent revival when our youngest kids started getting restless. It was fall on Cape Cod, and although the morning had begun at a crisp fifty degrees, I could already tell that we had overdressed in long sleeve shirts and pants.

"I'm thirsty," began our four-year-old.

"Me, too!" chimed in two of his older sisters.

"Do we have anything to drink?" All five kids began begging at once.

"Loooord," I moaned, beginning my own begging for the day, "It's too early in the day for this."

I had brought a toy bag, but because outside food was not allowed inside the tented area, I had left food and water in the car for our picnic lunch. What to do? I could walk back to the car, but it was a long walk, and the first speaker had just begun. I glanced around for a water fountain, but saw none. Begrudgingly, I went over to the concession stand and forked over two bucks for a bottle of spring water.

It's a small thing, but it really irritates me to have to buy water. I almost always carry a small, recycled soda bottle with me that I just keep refilling, because any place you go (at least in the U.S.), all the water you want is available for free from public water fountains or restrooms. To get a portable drink, all you need is a sanitary container; a bottle, a cup, or even a plastic bag will work. The real rub at the conference was that right next to the concession stand was an unlimited source of free water from the sinks in the restrooms. Therefore, to satisfy my children's thirst, what I really needed was a clean vessel, not water. The water was already there.

An apt spiritual parallel occurred to me as I walked toward the bathroom to refill my two-dollar plastic bottle for the first of many times that day: clean vessels are what God really needs to carry his love to a dry and thirsty world. God is already here! God is the source of Living Water, free and overflowing. As Jesus told the woman at the well, "Every one who drinks of this water will thirst again, but whoever drinks of the water that I shall give him will never thirst; the water that I shall give him will become in him a spring of water welling up to eternal life." (John 4:13).

How often has a child of mine (or a friend) come to me with a thirst to be loved, or a thirst to know God better, or a thirst for an understanding that would help them solve a problem, and I've tried to manufacture some water to satisfy their thirst? Too many times. "If I could only say the right thing, recommend the right book, or point them to the right Scripture verse," I'd convince myself, "then their thirst would be satisfied, their questions answered, and their desires fulfilled."

How wrong I was! It is not possible for me to create the kind of water that would satisfy their true thirst. All I really need to be is a clean vessel that God can use. 1 Corinthians 6:19 reads like this: "Do you not know that your body is the temple of the Holy Spirit within you, which you have from God? You are not your own; you were bought with a price."

As Christians, we are like those recycled water bottles. Jesus bought us for the price of his death on the cross. When we are baptized in him, we are cleansed, purified from original sin, and filled with the Holy Spirit for the first time. Through ongoing repentance, we are washed clean of actual sin and capable of being recycled or refilled with his living water.

As the woman at the well—and this woman at the concession stand—found out, Jesus is the Living Water. Our part in quenching the spiritual thirst of our children is to be a purified vessel that the Lord can use, empty of ourselves but full of Living Water.

Growing Spiritually This Week

1. Get a glass of water. Explore the water with your five senses, and then write a list of all its merits and qualities. What role does water play in sustaining life on earth?

2. Read John 4:1–29. What happened between verses 7 and 29 to transform the woman at the well into a useful vessel for God? In what ways have you encountered Jesus, the Living Water, in a transforming manner?

3. It what ways have you tried to be the water instead of a vessel for God's use in helping family and friends when they have physical and

spiritual thirst? What are some practical ways you could be God's vessel instead?

4. Write out 1 Corinthians 6:19–20 in your journal. What does it mean to glorify God in your body? In your spirit? In what way do your body and your spirit belong to God?

DRIVING LESSONS

Well, it finally happened; our oldest child got her driver's license. For the first time ever, she and her next younger brother drove out the driveway and headed to high school without my husband or me on board. Their faces were beaming. If the car could have shared their emotions, it would have flown.

For our very first driving lesson last winter, my daughter and I went to a quiet industrial park near our house. It was a safe place for her to practice the rules of the road that she had learned in her driver's education class. I drove to the park, we switched seats, and she drove around the empty streets. It was a rather humorous time as she learned how to gently apply the brakes, and I learned just how well my seatbelt worked. After driving in many different circles, we switched seats, and I drove home.

We continued in this pattern until it became clear to me that, although she knew all the rules, without any traffic on the roads she wasn't going to learn the importance of following the rules. Taking a deep breath, I told her to exit the park and drive home. I was relatively calm on the outside until I saw a huge cement mixer careening toward us around a bend. It wasn't my life but my hands that flashed before me as I white-knuckled the dashboard, wishing with all my heart that they were on the steering wheel. My daughter, however, turned the steering wheel gently, stayed squarely in her own lane, and we did not die. During a subsequent driving lesson, three young bikers swerved from the side of the road into our lane. Once again my hands flashed in front of me, but she calmly handled that challenge, too, and another driving lesson passed without any mishaps.

I have discovered so many spiritual applications to those driving lessons. The most obvious one is that it's easy enough to know all the rules of driving; it's quite another thing to know how to apply them when we are actually behind the wheel. Life is the same way. We can memorize the entire Bible and The_Catechism of the Catholic Church so that on a written test we would look quite skilled, but head knowledge is not what faith is all about. The reason for learning rules like the Ten Commandments is so that we can walk out of Mass—or drive out of our industrial parks—and apply our learning to our living, where the stakes are real (and high), for better or worse.

A Scripture passage from James proclaims that a faith that produces good works is a faith that is working, and a working faith is one that makes a tangible difference in the world. "What does it profit, my brethren, if a man says he has faith but has not works? Can his faith save him? If a brother or sister is ill-clad and in lack of daily food, and one of you says to them, 'Go in peace, be warmed and filled,' without giving them the things needed for the body, what does it profit? So faith by itself, if it has no works, is dead" (James 2:14–17).

We cannot stay safely uninvolved in the messiness of the world around us forever, and neither can our children. Even with adequate training and practice in the Catholic faith, the time will come for each of us to venture out of our safe church pews and prayer corners in order to get involved. St. James says that by staying safely away from people who are needy or inconvenient, we may actually risk our own salvation. Faith without works is dead. It seems that, although the road of life may contain bosses as intimidating as cement trucks and relatives as unpredictable as kids riding bikes, we can't hide away from them forever. Keeping a firm yet gentle grip on our faith in Jesus, we must steer ourselves squarely into the tangle of it all in order to "go into all the world and preach the gospel to the whole creation" (Mark 16:15).

Growing Spiritually This Week

1. Who taught you how to drive a car? What do you remember about those lessons? Draw a picture of your very first car, or write a detailed description of it.

2. When did you receive your first lessons about the Catholic faith? About the Bible? Who taught you these lessons? In what ways have these lessons adequately prepared you to drive on the highway of life? In what ways have they not?

3. Read James 2:14–26. By what is faith made perfect? By what is man justified? In order to be animated or fully alive, what does faith need? How would you describe an animated, fully alive faith?

4. Recall a time when you successfully applied your learning about the Catholic faith to your living the Catholic faith. How did this come about? How could you use that as a pattern for future experiences?

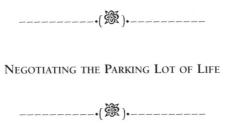

Negotiating the Parking Lot of Life

Teaching my sixteen-year-old daughter how to drive reminded me just how dangerous parking lots are. Trucks crisscross in every direction. Pedestrians walk wherever they want. Few drivers feel obligated to follow the customary "rules of the road." How is one supposed to teach a new driver to drive safely in an environment where there are no hard-and-fast rules? Medium-sized parking lots that have no clearly painted parking spots, no rights-of-way, and multiple exits and entrances are the worst. He or she who honks the loudest reigns supreme. Sakes alive, just give me regular roads with posted speed limits, stoplights, and lane markings!

The same question applies to releasing our maturing children into today's society where there are no hard-and-fast moral rules. How do we teach them to live safely in a society where moral relativism reigns supreme? Living in such a society is as dangerous as driving at a high speed in a mall parking lot the day after Thanksgiving. Thankfully, however, we are Catholic, so there is hope.

The *Catechism of the Catholic Church* calls all laypersons "to seek the kingdom of God by engaging in temporal affairs and directing them according to God's will" (*CCC*, #898). The world gives so much negative press to the basic tenets of our faith, presenting them as rigid decrees from Rome that hold us "good Catholics" back from really enjoying life to the fullest, but it's simply not true. Directing all things according to God's will by following the guidelines of the Church is what gives us the freedom to enjoy truly wonderful things like healthy marriages, harmonious homes, and happy kids in this life—and eternal happiness with God our Father in the next one.

The moral and ethical rules given to us by God in holy Scripture, and from God through holy men and women of the Church, are given for our own good. They are like street signs, median lines, and speed limits that are posted to keep drivers safe, not simply because some higher-up thought it would be fun to cramp our style of driving or living. Making simple family rules—bedtimes for young ones, curfews for older ones, finishing one's plate at a meal, and enforcing consequences for willfully breaking these rules —lays the foundation for teaching our kids life's more important rules—modesty in dress and in speech, diligence in school, honesty in the workplace, and chastity in dating and marriage. Rules like these accomplish the same end for families as the rules of the road do for drivers: they protect us from harm, guide us in negotiating tricky relationships, and may even prevent our hair from going gray prematurely. (Okay, I made that last one up, but I'm serious about the rest!) Would we teach our teen drivers to ignore a street sign that says, "Bridge Closed to Unauthorized Traffic?" No, of course we wouldn't. So why would we ignore (and thereby teach our kids to ignore) a Church sign that says, "Sexual Activity Closed to Unmarried Persons" or "Assisted Suicide Closed to People of All Ages?" Living and teaching such ignorance would be putting our souls and their souls in mortal danger.

In the 1970s song, "Big Yellow Taxi," Joni Mitchell (and more recently the Counting Crows) sings, "They paved paradise and put up a parking lot." Whether Ms. Mitchell meant it or not, that verse is perfect for our parking lot to life analogy. Paradise is a state of being where everything is ordered to the glory of God. If we rip up, throw out, and pave over all that godly order, we are left with impermeable emptiness and chaos: a parking lot. If we live by the posted rules of the Catholic faith, no matter how the world around us is living, we are helping to bring about God's full and glorious kingdom here on earth: in a word, *paradise*. Showing our kids how to direct their lives according to God's will—how to follow the life-giving rules of the Church—is how we keep not only their bodies but also their mortal souls safe in the parking lot of life.

Growing Spiritually This Week

1. Are you a natural rule follower, or natural rule breaker? When confronted with something like a "No Turn on Red" traffic sign, for example, are you inclined to obey, or do you check to see if there are any police around—and if not, turn anyway? What if you are in a hurry?

2. What sorts of rules did you have in your family of origin? What happened if you broke the rules? List some of the rules you have instituted for your children and the purpose of each rule. What happens if your children break these house rules?

3. When confronted with the moral and ethical rules of holy Scripture and the Catholic Church, are you naturally inclined to obey them or question them? In what areas of life are you tempted to think that the Church is just a cosmic killjoy? In what areas do you agree that the Church's teachings keep us safe and oriented toward the good of all?

4. Design a parking lot to take your children from the entrance gate of having good friends; through the next stages of dating, courting, being engaged, getting married; and finally to the exit gate of having a faith-filled family of their own. Use signs, traffic lights, and pavement painting to safely direct their driving through potential hazards along the way.

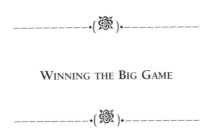

Winning the Big Game

In an innovative effort to catechize parents, a mini-retreat called Pre-Jordan is given at our parish for parents asking to have their child baptized. It is a wonderful retreat with only one problem as far as I can tell: many parents feel coerced into coming. Some dads don't even try to conceal their "I'm only here because she dragged me" attitude.

During the years we were part of the team for this ministry, my husband and I gave a talk titled "Raising Catholic Kids." Attempting to build a bridge to parents with either faltering or completely forgotten Catholic faith, my husband opened our talk by asking, "How many of you played sports as kids?" Nearly all the hands in the room flew up. More importantly, however, the lights went on in their eyes.

As my husband continued asking questions like, "Were you particularly good at any one sport? Did you win any championships?" I started tossing mountains of sports equipment into the audience. At this point in our talk, I could see questions flashing across the participants' faces...questions like "Are we in the wrong class?" "Weren't we here for something about the Church?"

This kind of convenient compartmentalization of our faith has infected many Catholics today. We can talk easily about sports with just about anyone, but only clumsily about our faith even with immediate family. It's not so surprising. It is a symptom of trying to live in a culture that is largely hostile to Catholicism, but it is not the way Jesus intended us to live. The New Testament tells us that Jesus spent his time on earth showing his disciples that his number one objective for humanity was for us to enjoy eternal life with him in heaven. If eternal life is our ultimate victory, then going to church, reading Scripture, and loving our neighbor constitute our daily practices, our ways of staying in shape for the "Big Game."

"The connection between sports and Church is love," my husband and I told the Pre-Jordan audience. "What you love you will pass on to your children. It's as easy as that." Moreover, my husband and I proposed that raising Catholic kids is not any more complex than sharing our love for a sport (or any other activity) with our children. Our children experience our faith, our love of Jesus and his Church, and they copy it. As they grow older, we provide everything they will need to grow in their own faith—prayers, Christian media, CCD or Catholic schooling, and retreats—in the same way that we provide what they will need to improve their own athletic abilities—baseball gloves, swim goggles, coaches, and camps.

One of the biggest blessings to my husband and me as Pre-Jordan team members was that most parents left feeling rejuvenated, even if they arrived reluctantly. At the end of the retreat, the most pressing question from parents was, "How do we make time to revive and exercise our own faith and to take part as a family in all the regular Catholic spiritual practices?"

"Easy," we'd say, "we do it the same way we carve time out of our busy schedule to watch the Patriots play a postseason game, go to the gym, or coach a soccer team. In the case of sports, we make the time because of our love of the game. In the case of our faith, we make the time because of our love for Jesus. We make the time because our kids learn more with their eyes than with their ears when it comes to knowing what is important to us. Once our personal love of Jesus is in place and in practice, everything else about raising Catholic kids falls in line rather naturally."

As a Catholic parent, your ultimate goal for your children is the same goal as Jesus has for you. It is not that they become sports stars, get into an Ivy League college, or have lucrative careers and loving families, but that they would share eternal life with God—and that is a goal that every man, woman, and child has the potential to achieve.

Growing Spiritually This Week

1. Did you play sports as a child? Were you involved in any other activities that you seriously loved? What did you love about those sports or activities? Do you still participate in these sports or activities today? Why would or wouldn't you support your children in participating in these activities?

2. What do you love about the Catholic faith? During what faith-based activities do you feel most like a valued member of Team Catholic, coached and encouraged to play well by the hierarchy and by fellow parishioners?

3. How do you put your faith into practice daily? Weekly? Annually?

4. Choose your favorite sport, and create a "fantasy" team from the members of your family. Who's the coach? Who's the team captain? Who's on offense, who's on defense, and why?

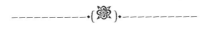

THE POWER-PACKED BODY AND BLOOD OF JESUS

As I was running through the garage, stuffing any and all manner of sports equipment into several bags, I instinctively grabbed a Power Bar and a bottle of Gatorade. No, my husband and I weren't headed to a sports game; we were on our way to church to deliver the sports-themed talk that I wrote about in the previous reflection.

Upon arrival at the parish hall this particular evening, I began unpacking my sports bags. Pulling out the Power Bar and the Gatorade, I laughed to myself. As a part of the evening, we always enjoyed a fully catered, mouthwatering Italian meal, so I wouldn't need either prepackaged energy source that night. As I looked at the two items in my hand, wondering what to do with them, the Holy Spirit gave me a profound insight.

Perhaps the insight about nourishment came to me so unmistakably because the aroma of garlic and basil was already wafting through the parish hall, but when I looked at the items in my hands, I unexpectedly saw the Power Bar as the Body of Christ and the bottle of Gatorade as the Blood of Christ. What I actually held in my hands was health food, specially formulated to keep active athletes healthy and strong, but what I truly saw were images of the host and the cup of wine—soul food especially consecrated to keep active Catholics healthy and strong. Boy, did I blink and try to refocus my eyes!

As a mom, I know that if my young athletes don't keep their blood sugar up and stay hydrated, they risk burning out in the middle of a game. I had never before thought of any of us needing the spiritual nourishment of the Eucharist just as urgently, lest we burn out in the middle of our faith lives, but it made sense immediately. Understanding the physical benefits of carb-packed Power Bars and electrolyte-rich bottles of Gatorade to our bodies, it isn't much of a stretch to understand the spiritual benefits of the divinely enriched, consecrated Bread and Wine of the Mass to our souls.

So overwhelmed was I by my new desire to provide for my kids' spiritual nourishment with the same diligence that I provide for their physical nourishment, that I replaced much of my talk that night with this new insight. I was grateful to be able to share with the participants that we never stop learning how to be better Catholic parents; if we had given them an idea or two about raising Catholic children, we had been successful in giving them a start, but no more. To go the distance in their own faith and in raising their child to be a faith-filled Catholic, what they urgently needed to understand was that baptism is only the beginning.

Similar to the way that many sports are divided into innings or quarters, the community process of becoming born again as a child of God in the Catholic Church takes place during three distinct sacraments of Christian initiation. We receive these in order: baptism, holy Communion, and confirmation (see *CCC*, #1212). Like good athletes that listen attentively to their coaches, we too should listen attentively to the Church when she says that none of these sacraments is a stand-alone event, but rather part of a whole life of faith. We need to press on toward receiving these (and all the sacraments) on our way to becoming varsity members of the Catholic Church.

Growing Spiritually This Week

1. What measures do you take to be sure your family develops and maintains healthy eating habits? Can you remember a time when a steady diet of unhealthy food brought on negative consequences? When healthy eating brought on positive consequences?

2. Read John 6:47–51. Our Catholic belief that the Eucharist is truly Jesus' flesh and blood in the form of bread and wine is based on Jesus' teaching in this Scripture. To what other miraculous bread does Jesus refer in this passage? How is the Eucharist different from that bread?

3. Read Matthew 26:26–29. During what event did Jesus say these words? What is the new covenant to which Jesus is referring? Why does he say his blood will be shed? When will we next drink from the blood of the covenant with Jesus?

4. The sacraments of initiation in the Catholic Church are baptism, first Communion, and confirmation. How would you say that these three work together—like innings, quarters, or halves—to represent the whole game of our life of faith? What parts do the other sacraments (reconciliation, anointing of the sick, marriage, and holy orders) play in the whole game?

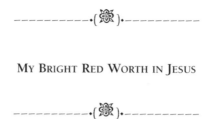

My Bright Red Worth in Jesus

The other day, I fell into a pit of despair. Okay, honestly, I didn't fall. I wasn't even pushed. I flung myself in! I had been wrestling for weeks over a decision about cocurricular activities for one of my kids, and before I knew it, I had reached the end of my emotional rope. So I jumped headlong into the rocky pit of despair, and I had a nice little breakdown. It wasn't so much the circumstances as the feelings they were causing me to have that threw me over the brink—feelings of inadequacy, feelings of having failed my child, meaning that as a mom I was worthless, a total wash up. In the midst of my carrying on, the Holy Spirit visited me with a word picture.

He brought to my mind a game I used to play with the kids when we lived in Berkeley, California. During those years, on the way to school we would drive over the crest of Albany Hill, where for a few seconds we could see the Golden Gate Bridge about ten miles out across San Francisco Bay. As we drove up the hill, the kids and I would guess what color the bridge would be that day. Our game may sound funny to you, because if you know anything about the Golden Gate Bridge, you probably know it is fire-engine red. So why would we be guessing its color?

Well, from across San Francisco Bay, the Golden Gate Bridge very rarely looked red. In fact, its appearance changed by the hour. Two factors were involved: one was the weather, and the other was the angle of the sun. If there were any fog or clouds between the bridge and us, it could appear to be pinkish or even purple with the sun shining on it in the morning. If the sky were clear blue in the morning, we would see the bridge as it truly was and celebrate a rare "bright red bridge" day. When we drove home in the later part of the day, the sun was behind the bridge, and it always appeared as a silhouette in some shade of black, gray, blue, or purple depending, again, on the weather conditions. Some days, we couldn't see the bridge at all because of the thick fog.

As I was lying there, wallowing in my pit of despair, the Holy Spirit seemed to be saying that my emotions were affecting me just like the weather and the sun affected the appearance of the Golden Gate Bridge. My emotions were causing me to experience feelings that did not reflect reality.

I climbed out and sat on the edge of my pit. "No matter how it appears from a distance, the Golden Gate Bridge is bright, fire-engine red," I reassured myself. And the truth was that my child was fine! I was fine. We were experiencing some challenges in the coordination of cocurricular activities, but I had allowed my emotions to color the situation to the point of believing that not only had I failed my child, but that I, personally, was a failure. My emotions had completely blocked out reality.

With great relief, I straightened up and walked away from my pit (truth be told, it was really just my bed, pillows being easier on my head than rocks). The Golden Gate Bridge game reminded me of the bright red reality that when things don't work out just right (or even if they go terribly wrong) in our lives, it does not mean that we, personally, are failures. We are created in God's image, women and men for whom Jesus came to earth, died, and rose again. Tomorrow will bring new challenges and more emotions trying to color, minimize, or completely block out our identity and self-worth in Christ. Calling to mind the true, fire-engine red color of the Golden Gate Bridge reminds us that, no matter how real or intense they appear, our emotions don't always reflect reality.

Growing Spiritually This Week

1. Think of an object that does not always have the same appearance: a window, a campfire, the surface of a lake, or anything else that appears differently at different times of the day. What conditions cause the appearance of the object to change? Does the material essence of that object actually change? Why or why not?

2. Read Genesis 1:26. If no two human beings were, are, or ever will be completely identical, what can it mean that all people are made in the image and likeness of God? What does this mean for you?

3. Have you ever felt like a failure as a person instead of as a person who simply failed at a certain activity? Why did you feel this way? Read Jeremiah 31:3. How does God look at you? Does God consider your physical appearance, intelligence, wealth, or anything else before gazing upon you with love? How easily do you accept this love from God?

4. Recall a time when feelings ran high, and you mistook the appearance of a behavior or of an event for the reality of what was going on. What conditions caused this to happen? How could you have known the reality of the situation, instead of only the appearance?

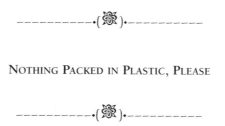

NOTHING PACKED IN PLASTIC, PLEASE

By mid-October, Thanksgiving and Christmas items begin crowding out Halloween in the center aisle of the grocery store. It exhausts me just looking at it. As twenty-first–century American Catholics, we live under the shadow of a commercial, media-driven culture that feeds us the never-ending message that we need more, more, MORE! There is so much racing around, pursuing goals, acquiring goods, and checking off lists. Commercials, billboards, and junk mail bombard us with the message that satisfaction in life is not possible until we have this or that new and "best" thing. No price is too high, no sacrifice too great. Of course, the problem is that there is always another new and "best" thing.

Our obsession for more doesn't stop with material goods, either. Rampant consumerism pollutes our thinking at just about every level. It slyly coos, "Oh, so you have a job. That's nice, but did you know that for just a little longer commute your neighbor has a job that pays a lot more? Plus, her company? Well, it's the leader in the industry."

I'd love to tell you that I'm above such media-driven consumerism, but it would be a lie. As much as all of us may want to deny the influence of our more-and-bigger-are-better society, we all fall victim to its hooks at times. We fall victim because there is a kernel of truth in its message. We should pursue our dreams. We should attempt the heights we were born to climb. We should want good things for our families and loved ones. But when does all our pursuing, acquiring, and striving become merely "chasing after the wind," as Ecclesiastes 4:4 describes meaningless labor? When do we stop breaking our necks, bending the rules, and shifting our priorities in order to achieve goals that the world—not God—has set up for us? How do we recognize the boundary between the life goals we were meant to achieve and chasing after the wind?

St. Paul instructs us in the fine points of doing this in Romans 12:2: "Do not be conformed to this world but be transformed by the renewal of your mind, that you may prove what is the will of God, what is good and acceptable and perfect." If we haven't figured it out by reading the life and times of Jesus Christ in the Gospels, St. Paul tells it like it is in his letter to the Romans: being a Christian is being radically different from the world at large. To be a Christian means to stop conforming and start transforming our lives.

Where the world offers us a million self-help books, we should first buy, study, read, and digest the wisdom of the Bible and the Catechism of the Catholic Church. Scripture and the Catechism are our signposts, pointing the way to God's good, perfect, and pleasing will for us. Scripture and the Catechism are our escorts to and through the essential truths of the Catholic faith. Before needing a therapist or a recovery group, we should preemptively get God's help with our problems by attending Mass, going to regular confession, and establishing a time to read our Bible and pray daily. Hebrews 4:12–16 says: "For the word of God [Scripture] is living and active, sharper than any two-edged sword, piercing to the division of soul and spirit, of joints and marrow, and discerning the thoughts and intentions of the heart." Scripture is powerful. Scripture will help us know when we have crossed the line between the life goals we were meant to achieve and merely chasing after the wind.

As the months roll around and a new seasonal items invade the center aisle of our grocery stores, maybe we can take one small step away from the consumer pattern of the our world and not rush to buy anything. Instead, we can remind ourselves that our spiritual hunger will not be satisfied and our souls will not be saved by the acquisition of anything packed in plastic. Only by accepting the gift of faith from the Lord Jesus Christ will our souls be satisfied and saved, and that gift is free for the asking.

Growing Spiritually This Week

1. As a child, what were some of your dreams and ambitions? As a teenager? As an adult? As a spouse and/or parent? If these have changed, what caused them to change?

2. Read Romans 12:2, then look up the words "transform" and "conform" in the dictionary. What are the essential differences between the two verbs? Which did Jesus do?

3. Read Hebrews 4:12–16. According to this verse, how can the Word of God help you stop chasing the wind and start transforming your life as a believer in Christ?

4. Draw a picture in your journal of someone who is literally or figuratively trying to "chase the wind." What is that person's attitude

toward their activity? What is the look on their face? Draw a person who is fruitfully engaged in God's work for them. What is this person's attitude? The look on their face?

Keeping It Simple

Jesus was the master of simplicity. He took the Ten Commandments, reduced them to two, and still covered the same moral ground. Faced with the need to feed five thousand hungry men and their families on a windy Galilean hillside, Jesus didn't start calculating the outrageous amount of food or money he would need to satisfy everyone. He simply prayed in thanksgiving for the available food—five loaves of bread and two fish—and started passing it around.

Jesus was a reductionist. He had the divine ability to cut through centuries of complex and competing rules, laws, and expectations and get right to the heart of the matter, no matter what the matter was. Jesus didn't recommend that his followers swear by heaven, by anywhere on earth, or even by their own honor. He said, "Let what you say be simply 'Yes' or 'No'; anything more than this comes from evil" (Matthew 5:37). When it came to advising his followers about how to spend and how to save their time, talent, and treasure, Jesus covered all the bases by saying, "Do not lay up for yourselves treasures on earth, where moth and rust consume and where thieves break in and steal, but lay up for yourselves treasures in heaven, where neither moth nor rust consumes and where thieves do not break in and steal. For where your treasure is, there will your heart be also" (Matthew 6:19–20).

No matter with whom or what Jesus was dealing, he had this easy ability to remain uncomplicated and loving. How I envy that ability! I love to read about famous people who reflected it, like St. Francis of Assisi and Bl. Teresa of Calcutta. Even more so, I love to be with people who live uncomplicated love like my two unmarried aunts who have spent their lives caring for my grandmothers. These people are what they seem to be. They do not play mind games or try to work the system. They do not wear their faith on the outside like actresses wearing glittering gowns at the Academy Awards. They have a deeper beauty that is revealed by the sparkle in their eyes and the ready smile on their faces. They are what I call "simply Christian," and they are my ultimate role models.

Maybe it's our fallen nature, but it has been my experience that simply Christian people are hard to find. Perhaps it is because being simply Christian is not all that simple. In fact, it takes real effort and divine assistance. After reading what Jesus said about not storing up earthly treasures and to help myself grow in simple Christianity, I dreamed up something like a hope chest in heaven that is mine to fill. My heavenly hope chest is a big, beautiful box, fashioned from cherry- and almond-colored woods. Its surface is silky smooth, the kind a child's fingers instinctively reach out to touch. The inside is lined with fresh-smelling cedar and contains many triangle-shaped compart-ments. My heavenly hope chest gives me a place to "put" virtuous acts of patience, hope, love, or modesty. Having this chest makes more tan-gible the somewhat elusive idea of storing up heavenly treasure and helps me to think about the "heart of the matter" when I need to decide how to spend or to store up my time, talent, and treasure.

What a wonderful family activity it would be to have everyone envision and draw his or her heavenly treasure chest. Perhaps a man would picture his heavenly treasure box more as a toolbox or tackle box. A child might think of a toy box or pirate's chest. A woman might imagine a wicker basket or an upright wardrobe. A drawing of each person's treasure chest could be displayed somewhere in the house as a reminder to him or her to choose simple, loving behaviors that hold their value in heaven over earthly possessions that moths and rust can destroy. Ultimately, I think the virtues we deposit in our heavenly treasure chests will lead us not only to our own hearts but also to the heart of Jesus, the master of simplicity.

Growing Spiritually This Week

1. Make a list of people, well-known or not, whom you would call "simply Christian." What personal characteristics or attitudes make them this way?

2. Sit in silence for a bit today, asking the Holy Spirit to help you develop an image of your perfect heavenly treasure box. If possible, draw a full color picture of this treasure box in your journal.

3. Draw or make a list of the items filling your heavenly treasure box, and then read Matthew 6:19–20. According to this verse, what is the most important item in your treasure box? How did it get there?

4. Conduct a ten-minute prayer blitz by saying (or writing) a list of absolutely everything for which you are grateful. Think of both big things and small things, complex things and simple things, and things that are personal, just to you.

MARY AND MARTHA FOR THE HOLIDAYS

Here's some news to increase the stress level of any woman out there: Thanksgiving is close at hand, and Christmas is only one month after that. For days that are most often billed as joyful celebrations filled with family togetherness, the upcoming holidays sometimes become just another acceptable opportunity to get stressed. It does not have to be this way, however. Holiday get-togethers with family and friends can also present us with the perfect opportunities to work on our "inner Mary" and our "inner Martha."

With this phrase, I am of course alluding to the famous set of biblical sisters, Mary and Martha. It is recorded in the Gospels that Jesus visited these sisters and their brother Lazarus on more than one occasion. It is, perhaps, for this reason, that in Luke 10:38–42, Martha appears to have become so close with Jesus as to have completely lost her appreciation for who he was. Instead of demonstrating awe and admiration of Jesus, Martha begins complaining about her sister, Mary. In the process of hosting a dinner for Jesus and his disciples, "Martha was distracted by all the preparations that had to be made. She came to him and asked, 'Lord, don't you care that my sister has left me to do the work by myself? Tell her to help me!'"

Wow! Can you even imagine? To welcome the Lord Jesus into your home and immediately involve him in a sibling dispute? Well, Jesus was savvy enough not to get caught in the middle of a squabble between sisters. "'Martha, Martha,' the Lord answered, '"you are anxious and troubled about many things; one thing is needful. Mary has chosen the good portion, which shall not be taken away from her'" (verses 41–42).

Now, it has to be said that both sisters loved Jesus, and both were doing their best to serve him. As holiday hostesses, we need to have an "inner Martha" —a part of ourselves that is on the ball enough to do the bulk of the planning, shopping, decorating, and cooking ahead of time. Jesus did not reprimand Martha for being concerned about the details. He simply pointed out that her priorities (and therefore her timing) were a little off. This story of family dynamics reveals the idea that true Christian hospitality is not measured in the quantity or quality of food served, the cleanliness of one's house, or the number of matching place settings and serving dishes one owns. True hospitality is measured by the amount of love offered and attention given, even if the guests are "only" our family members and close friends.

How long has it been (if ever) since we really looked at each member of our family and saw a unique individual deserving of love—not because they are always so lovable, but because they are created in the image and likeness of God? Is it possible that, like Martha with Jesus, we have lost our sense of awe for our family members because we are in such close relationship with them? Could this be one reason why, instead of welcoming the upcoming holidays as opportunities to slow down, catch up, and reconnect with loved ones, we often only feel overwhelmed by the impending work of playing host to them?

Before Thanksgiving and Christmas are upon us, if we will ask God to help us see each of our family members and close friends as he sees them, I think we will be better able to embrace our "inner Mary"— that part of us which, like Mary with Jesus, can just sit down and listen when our guests arrive, even if all the details of the event are not in perfect order.

Mary and Martha represent two equally important ingredients of Christian hospitality: Martha beforehand; Mary in the midst. May all of us who are hosting family gatherings this Thanksgiving and Christmas be blessed with knowing when to call upon our inner Martha and when to send forth our inner Mary.

Growing Spiritually This Week

1. Have you ever tried to host the perfect holiday gathering? How did you feel during the preparation? During the event itself?

2. Read Luke 10:38–42. We've read about these two women before, but there is more to learn from their story. Who was in charge of the house where Jesus had dinner? Why did Jesus go there? In what ways did both women show their love for Jesus? To which sister can you most naturally relate? Why?

3. Was Jesus rebuking Martha for her concern about the household chores? If not, why was he rebuking her? Have you ever been to an event where the hostess was just too busy to spend time with you and the other guests? How did this make you feel?

4. In verse 42, Jesus says only one thing in needed. What is that thing? Begin today to pray for each of your family members by name, especially those whom you will see this holiday season. What else can you do to incorporate Jesus' "one thing" into your upcoming holiday gatherings?

BLESSED IS HE

The Sanctus prayer, or the "Holy, Holy, Holy," which is sung at Mass during the Eucharistic Prayer, is my personal favorite. As I prepare for the upcoming holiday season, one particular phrase from the Sanctus calms my nerves about getting together with family, friends, and/or coworkers who may not share my Catholic faith. That phrase is, "Blessed is he who comes in the name of the Lord," and it reminds me that I am called to be a blessing, even if others at the gathering are hostile toward my faith and my Church.

The holiday season starts with Thanksgiving, the national feast day recalling the three-day celebration that the Mayflower pilgrims enjoyed with the Wampanoag Indians who helped them survive that first grueling year in the New World. Some of the pilgrims, known as "separatists" back in England, came to this country in search of religious freedom as well as economic opportunity. As Catholics, we also have spiritual forefathers who came to the New World for religious and economic reasons.

About a hundred years before the pilgrims arrived in Plymouth, Catholic religious orders began sending priests to the New World to administer the sacraments to the Spanish and French explorers and teach the native people about Jesus Christ. Hindsight being 20/20, we can see that the intentions of the Europeans—missionaries included— were not always pure, and the results of their efforts were sometimes a mixed bag. When reading the history of our Catholic forefathers, how- ever, we discover that many truly came intending to be a blessing to the natives, and they often endured great hardship and martyrdom for their efforts. The story of one Spanish Jesuit, Fr. Eusebio Kino, especially captures my imagination.

Father Kino was an Italian-born missionary during the late 1600s to the early 1700s. He ministered to native tribes in what is now known as the American Southwest, founding twenty-nine missions in twenty- five years and traveling thousands of miles across desert lands. Following the standard Jesuit plan of evangelization, Fr. Kino would first enter a native village with armed guards and request permission to live among the people. If permission were granted, he would move into the village and spend the next several years learning the native tongue. Only after he had learned the language and the customs of the tribe and had gained their trust did he begin to share the Good News.

Fr. Kino's plan of spreading the Good News is one we can emulate when gathering with the potentially hostile natives of our own tribes this holiday season:

- We need to enter peaceably, but armed with the knowledge of the truth of the Gospel and capable of defending ourselves and our faith if necessary.

- We should send our ears to the gathering before our tongues. Listening before talking builds others up and paves the way for trust.
- Finally, over time our actions will open the door for us to share the Good News. When that door opens, it won't help for us to get on a soapbox, but instead simply share the blessings of the faith life from our personal experience.

St. Francis, founder of the Franciscan order which sent hundreds of missionaries to the New World, is credited with giving some of the best advice on how to be a blessing to others: "Preach the Gospel wherever you go; if necessary, use words." In other words, at holiday gatherings, we can be a blessing by our actions. We can help with the cooking and cleaning, get up a game of ball with any restless young natives, and give their mothers a break. We also need to realize that, because few families, neighbors, or coworkers are completely united in their faith lives, holiday conflicts are inevitable. Also realize that, just like our Catholic forefathers, our motives for interacting with the assembled "tribe" will be mixed. Consequently, our results will be mixed too, but we don't have to sweat it. All we need to do is just keep reminding ourselves, "Blessed is he who comes in the name of the Lord."

Growing Spiritually This Week

1. What do you think it means to be a blessing to someone? Has anyone ever been a blessing to you under somewhat trying circumstances? How did they accomplish this?
2. Read all of Psalm 118 and write verses 26 and 27 in your journal. What has the psalmist's life been like? Record all the reasons why the

psalmist is nonetheless praising God. What is the psalmist's heart attitude toward God?

3. Read Matthew 28:16–20. In this passage we find Jesus' final instructions on what to do with all he taught and the salvation he won for all humankind. How comfortable are you with sharing the Good News in your own corner of the world, at your own dinner table, with your own family members? What assurance does Jesus give us in the last sentence of this passage?

4. Reread the steps Fr. Kino used to open the doors to sharing the Gospel with native peoples in the early American Southwest. Brainstorm some tangible ways to mimic these steps and be a blessing to specific family members, neighbors, and coworkers this holiday season.

ABOUT THE AUTHOR

Heidi Bratton is an award-winning photographer and author with a gift for bringing simple truths to life in a practical way for adults and children alike. Heidi is a regular columnist for Catholic Exchange.com, FaithandFamilyLive.com, CatholicMom.com, and *The Anchor* diocesan newspaper. Heidi has written over twenty books, including her four newest children's board books, the *Celebrate* series. Heidi and her husband, John, have six children ranging in age from two to twenty and live in Ann Arbor, Michigan.